The Sisters' Guide to
IN-DEPTH BIBLE STUDY

Victoria L. Johnson

InterVarsity Press
Downers Grove, Illinois

InterVarsity Press
P.O. Box 1400, Downers Grove, IL 60515-1426
World Wide Web: www.ivpress.com
E-mail: mail@ivpress.com

InterVarsity Press® is the book-publishing division of InterVarsity Christian Fellowship/USA®, a student movement active on campus at hundreds of universities, colleges and schools of nursing in the United States of America, and a member movement of the International Fellowship of Evangelical Students. For information about local and regional activities, write Public Relations Dept., InterVarsity Christian Fellowship/USA, 6400 Schroeder Rd., P.O. Box 7895, Madison, WI 53707-7895, or visit the IVCF website at <www.ivcf.org>.

Cover design and interior art: Cindy Kiple

Cover image: kenta cloth: The Newark Museum/Art Resource, NY
        hand on Bible, glasses on Bible: Eyewire Collection/Getty Images
        woman with braids: Digital Vision/Getty Images
        woman with spiral perm: Jim Arbogast/Getty Images
        woman with earring: Ryan McVay/Getty Images
        left profile of woman: Tim Hall/Getty Images

ISBN 0-8308-2049-3

Printed in the United States of America ∞

Library of Congress Cataloging-in-Publication Data

Johnson, Victoria L. Saunders.
   The sisters' guide to in-depth Bible study / Victoria Johnson.
     p. cm.
Rev. ed. of: Bible study for busy women. Detroit, MI: Dabar Pub.,
©1998.
Includes bibliographical references.
   ISBN 0-8308-2049-3 (pbk.: alk. paper)
  1. Bible—Study and teaching. 2. Christian women—Religious life. I.
Johnson, Victoria L. Saunders. Bible study for busy women. II. Title.
   BS600.3.J64 2003
   220'.071'5—dc21
                                              2002156378

P	17	16	15	14	13	12	11	10	9	8	7	6	5	4	3	2	1
Y	15	14	13	12	11	10	09	08	07	06	05	04	03				

This book is lovingly dedicated to my friend,

REBECCA FLORENCE OSAIGBOVO,

a walking, talking example of a "living epistle."

Thanks for hanging in here with me all these years.

A friend loves at all times.

Proverbs 17:17

CONTENTS

Acknowledgments

To all of you who pray for me, give me words of encouragement, and help me in so many different ways—thank you. You know who you are.

Thanks to Cindy Bunch and the InterVarsity Press team. Let's hear it for the *kingdom risk takers!* You may not be able to see what we see through our African American Christian women's eyes, but you are willing to invest in our vision. Thank you for all you have done to work with me to accomplish this project.

A special thanks to Renee, Lucille and Abby. You are all more excited than I am about this Bible study method. That's precious. Thanks for reading the manuscript and giving your input. Renee, may you have many more spiritual babies. The ones you make are always so solid and reproductive. Mamma would be proud of you.

Thank you, Cedine Retreaters and Cedine Staff. Y'all got this "teach us how to do Bible study" ball rolling. Because of you this project became a book. I'll never forget that wonderful year of teaching at Cedine Bible Camp. Y'all prayed me through a tough year.

Thanks to all the women from the classes of Moody Bible Institute's Milwaukee extension. You were a constant reminder to me of how much women really love God's Word and really do want to be able to study it accurately and independently.

To Owaifo. Thanks for allowing Rebecca to be my friend and supporting so many of our crazy ideas. Thanks for all your help and investment in our writing and ministry ventures. Like we kept saying in Ethiopia, "What would we do without Owaifo?"

Thanks to the original *Bible Study for Busy Women* writing and publishing team. Your hard work is evident in this new book.

To Mary, Charlotte, Tony, Tina, Regina, Marsha, Lisa, the Tuesday Bible class, my natural hair experimental customers, the Living Waters leadership team, and some special people at Sojourner Truth House and Parklawn, especially the ladies in the church office. You all have prayed for me, have had confidence in me and have made me smile so many times. Thanks for being involved in my life, celebrating my writing gift and pushing me forward.

Thanks, Curtis, for continuing to be there for me and supporting me in your own way.

Thanks, Daddy and Mamma, James and Mattie Saunders. Happy fiftieth wedding anniversary—congratulations! May God give you fifty more Spirit-filled years. Thanks to my two sisters, Debra and Jamie. Thanks to all my extended family; you all continue to be my team of cheerleaders. Thanks so much.

To Lydia, Candacee and Andre, my three gifts from God. Thanks for putting up with a "crazy writer" mamma. Thank you, Lydia, for reminding me that I need to work harder and get my life in better shape. Thank you, Candacee, for telling me I work too much and need to take more walks out by the lake. You two balance me out well. And a special thank you to Andre for your little talk at McDonald's about getting more books out.

God used you to get me going again. All three of you truly amaze me.

And last and definitely not least, thanks to my Lord and Savior Jesus Christ. You keep reminding me that *you* are in control, even though things in my life seem so out of control. These last thirty plus years as a Christian have certainly been a ride I never dreamed of or imagined. But I can finally say like the old folks, "I wouldn't take anything for my journey now." I can see your hand in every detailed fabric of my life. Your handiwork is a marvel to behold. A special thank you for weaving in the ability to write. My heart sings in worship to you as you give me the words and I give them back to you. You are so wonderful to me!

PART ONE

Getting Motivated

1

Feastin' on Soul Food

A LETTER FROM JESUS

My dearly beloved Christian African American daughter,

*I love you. I have not forgotten you or those who came before you.
When your toes of color first hit these American shores, I knew.
I have seen every pain inflicted upon you. I know about every
injustice you have suffered in this country. Every tear every
African American woman has ever cried, I have in bottles in
heaven. I have not forgotten you. .*

*Like the women at my crucifixion, some of you have taken your
pain, your confusion and your anguish to the foot of my cross.
You've wept with them over my crucifixion and my death.*

*My African American daughter, you understand why I had to die.
You understood my Father's desire to be close to you. You know
your rebellious behaviors that caused the divine separation. While
they nailed me to the cross, you personally nailed your
wrongdoings.*

*Take the Bible into your hands, allowing its truth to permeate
your mind and fill your heart. Drink long and hard at my
fountain. You are thirsty and the water has been in God's Word all
this time. You are hot, tired and thirsty from your long journey.
Like the woman at the well, I have an appointment with you.
I know you. I have some things to say to you about your personal
situation that will heal you. Not only will I heal you but also like
the woman at the well you will run back to the city and tell your
family, your community and your world about me.*

*Open these pages of God's Word and drink deep from my fountain.
Know the rivers and streams of my love you have yet to
experience. Don't stop with just a cup; don't stop with just one*

plunge. Go daily and drink deeply. Let the rivers of my Word flow over you. Let it cleanse you from all that is not like me. Let it transform you into all that I am.

I long to clean out those closets and drawers that you have kept closed for years. Some of you don't even know they exist. Allow me to show you. Allow me to open the door. Though cleaning an infected wound is painful, I promise to be gentle and kind.

Oh, my African American daughters, I have so much more for you than you can ever think, dream or imagine (Ephesians 3:14-21).

Your true love awaits,

Jesus Christ

A few days before Thanksgiving in 1997, after seventeen years of marriage, my husband and I separated. It was one of the most devastating events of my life. I felt like a damsel in distress, sitting on the side of the road. My heart lay shattered on the ground, broken into a million pieces. My mind whirled with questions: "How can I pick up the pieces and go on? Lord, what do I do now?"

I felt like someone had died. But I knew that the morning would not bring a house full of family and friends to comfort me. There would be no mailbox full of sympathy cards with encouraging words. No long line of people waiting to deliver hugs. No twenty-dollar bills pressed into my hand. No flowers or fried chicken delivered to the house, nor a funeral and burial service to signal finality.

I had ministered to hurting women. Now it was my turn to cry—hard and long. For years the "African American woman's bad relationship pain" was a mystery to me. I married a wonderful Christian man, and we had three beautiful children. We struggled in our marriage from time to time, but usually things eventually worked out. I thought I had a marriage made in heaven. I envisioned my husband and I growing old and going on into eternity together. I could not understand why so many Christian couples separated. I use to say arrogantly, "They have Christ; why can't they keep it together?" Well, my sisters, "Miss Black Mary Poppins," one who thought that she had it all together, was about to have her parasol punched full of holes. I was about to learn a significant lesson in humility, empathy and compassion.

I cried and cried for several nights after my husband and I separated. But after I finally got a good night's sleep, I couldn't wait to study my Bible. Yes! Bible study! I couldn't wait to get alone with God and pull out my study Bible, with its Hebrew and Greek dictionaries, and grab a notebook and a pen. I longed to start studying words, looking up cross-references, and analyzing biblical history. I know it sounds crazy, but it's true!

BIBLE STUDY TO THE RESCUE

Over the years, I have found that deep personal *study* of God's Word, not just *reading* it, has moved me through several rough places in my life. If I was going to make it through the Thanksgiving and Christmas holidays, meet a book deadline that was a few months away, carry on my family responsibilities and continue to be emotionally stable, I had to *make* time for Bible study.

God himself met me during those times of study. It was as if he opened a door of hidden riches. He ushered me into a room wallpapered in gold and invited me to sit down at a banquet table loaded with delicious food. After I'd eaten, he surrounded me with praise music and we danced and sang. He spun me around the room, and we giggled and laughed. Each time he ordered me to end my study and commissioned me to share what I had experienced in this golden room with others. There were times I begged him to let me stay and just enjoy our time together. He assured me that I could always return. I committed my life to helping others discover the magnificence of God and the deep treasures in his Word.

This book is to help you experience the richness of studying the Bible. If you are new at Bible study, it will get you started. If you are an advanced student, it will motivate you and refresh your time in the Word. And if you are somewhere in between, it will give you plenty of help and suggestions. For those of you who are Bible study leaders I pray it will be a tool to help you help others.

Sisters, Bible study can become a solid anchor in our lives if we will let it. In the depressing times, when everything in our families, communities, churches and cities seems hopeless, in the midst of all of that, God wants to talk to us. If we would only believe and dig through the pages of Scripture, we will find the answers to our problems. As we study, we will start to discover wellsprings of sweet water for our thirsty souls. I hope to hear about you dancing hard and long with our magnificent Lord and Savior after your study time in God's Word.

If we make time to learn how to study the Bible and have the patience to allow God to bring this discipline to the point of joy, we will be able to sing, "The joy of the Lord is my strength," and really mean it. We would be able to say to ourselves, when Satan brings doubt, "God loves me." And we would know that not because of the song "Jesus Loves Me" we used to sing as children but because of the deep truths we have discovered in his Word.

I also believe a spiritual revival will sweep this country if more Christians study their Bibles and pray. These are two essentials if we are to know God in an intimate way and understand all that is available to us in Christ.

I pray that as you read through this book, you will not just learn another Bible study method that will be eventually be set aside. (Believe me, I have several collecting dust in my file cabinet.) My prayer is that as you learn how to dig deep into God's Word, it will become a gateway to usher you into the very presence of God. There you will find the help and grace to make it through the challenges of life.

A special invitation to men and women of other races: please read this book! Although many of the pictures, illustrations and stories address the sisters, I believe you can benefit from learning this method as well.

SOUL FEAST

Years ago Mrs. Sadie McCullum invited me and her nephew Clarence over to her house for dinner. Every inch of Sister McCullum's table was full of soul food. You name it, she cooked it, from fried chicken, turkey, dressing and not one but two kinds of greens, to pound cake and banana pudding. It was all there.

Clarence and I tried our best to eat as much as we could. That day I ate some of the best food I've ever tasted. But the best part of the meal was *not* the dressing seasoned just right or the desserts all baked with homemade ingredients. The best part of the meal was watching Mrs. McCullum watch us eat. She sat at the end of the table with the biggest smile across her face as we attempted to consume this gigantic meal. She was so-o-o-o glad to have cooked all this food for us. She knew we wouldn't be able to eat it all, but that didn't matter. She'd laugh and express so much joy every time we asked for another helping of cabbage or another slice of cornbread. She delighted to entertain us in her home, to share this meal with us. She was glad to see us eat it and enjoy.

When I reach for my Bible study tools, sit at the table or on my bed and dig into God's Word, I imagine my heavenly Father sitting with me and having the biggest smile on his face. When I'm going through difficult times and I reach for my Bible to listen to him speak, instead of reaching for the telephone to talk to one of my girlfriends, I imagine his smile. When I take the time to grapple with a word or phrase in the Bible, pray over it and go back and study again, I imagine his smile. When I attempt to listen to him through his Word when I'm confused or need guidance, I imagine God's smile.

God knows the Bible is a huge meal. We could never consume it all at once. There is so much to learn. But the main part of his joy is that we have decided to come and partake a meal with him. He desires for us to see the Word as not just something nutritious and healthy for us but something to thoroughly enjoy!

2

Beatin' the Bible Study Blues

Singing Those Bible Study Blues

Woke up this morning
Bible study on my mind
But Baby was downstairs cooking
And had my favorite breakfast done on time.

I got Bible study blues, baby.
I got those no good Bible study blues.

I finished my breakfast
Bible study on my mind
But Sally called and said
Sears got a 75% off sale and they open at nine.

I got Bible study blues, baby.
I got those no good Bible study blues.

I finished my Sears shopping
Bible study still on my mind
But my Baby said, "Let's go out to dinner
Cause that new dress got you lookin' so fine."

I got Bible study blues, baby.
I got those no good Bible study blues.

I got home from dinner
Bible study no longer on my mind
I pull up the cover and turn out the light
Lord, please forgive me, I'll see you when I rise and shine.

I got Bible study blues, baby.
I got those no good Bible study blues.

Victoria Johnson

The small Baptist church in which I grew up traditionally handed out Bibles to all sixth graders in the congregation. I vividly remember the day I received mine. We students all paraded up to the front of the church surrounded by a choir of loud Amens coming from the congregation. Mrs. Sinclair, the superintendent of the Sunday school, and Mr. Logue, the chairman of the Christian education department, each gave a brief speech. I don't remember exactly what either of them said, but I do remember Mr. Logue dabbing at the corner of his eye with his white handkerchief. Although he had given out many Bibles to sixth graders over the years, he got choked up each time. It was always a touching moment for him. His heart's desire for us was to read these Bibles and become knowledgeable about the Word of God.

I felt so proud as I walked back to my seat that Sunday, holding my white Bible with my name printed in gold letters on the front cover. I thought, *I am going to keep this Bible forever and read every single page, starting with Genesis.* I set a goal to read the entire Bible by the time I completed middle school.

THE CYCLE OF DEFEAT

With my motivation and determination, you'd expect that by the time I graduated from eighth grade my daily reading would have worn my new Bible out. Right? You'd expect that I would have easily reached my goal of finishing the book of Revelation by then. Right? *Wrong.* Guess again. By the time I completed middle school, I had no idea where to find that little white Bible with "Victoria L. Saunders" printed on the front cover in gold. I lost it somewhere between church, Granny's house and home. I not only lost the Bible, I lost interest in reading it. I never made it to the book of Revelation. I didn't even finish the book of Genesis.

I'm sad to say that this became my pattern with the Bible for the next twenty-five years: desire, disinterest, distraction and defeat.

Desire. I began Bible study with a heartfelt longing to read, study and know the Bible.

Disinterest. Failing to see the connection between the Word of God and the personal issues and challenges in my life, I involved myself in activities other than Bible study.

Distraction. I'd become preoccupied with these other activities, which I knew were not as important as Bible study but served to keep my days busy. Bible study was always on my list of things to do, but usually appeared at the bottom of the list.

Defeat. Eventually, because Bible study was not part of my daily schedule, I stopped reading the Bible altogether.

Every time I heard a sermon on the benefits of Bible study, the desire to go through the entire Bible would resurface in me again, just like when I received my first Bible. I would buy a new Bible or join a study group. Not long after, the points of the message would fade from my memory, the new Bible would find a place on the shelf with the rest of my Bible collection, and I would stop the study group. I was stuck in a cycle of defeat.

STUMBLING ALONG

For a long time, I was inconsistent in my study. I'd begin with a particular book of the Bible, determined to finish, but after a few weeks I'd drop it. Months would go by before I'd get back to it. Like a baby learning how to walk, I would take a few wobbly steps, fall and then sit on my bottom for a while. But like a baby determined to walk, I was determined to be a good Bible student.

Early in my Christian walk, leaders in my home church placed me in leadership and teaching positions. Although I had grown up in the church, I was ashamed of my lack of Bible knowledge. So I was firm in my resolve to keep studying and trying to understand the Bible, no matter how difficult it might be.

Victory! Something wonderful happened as I persistently studied the Bible. I began to discover the One who wrote the book. I realized his writings were love letters written personally to me.

> *Dear Victoria,*
> *You are on my mind and in my heart.*
> *I love you,*
> *Your heavenly Father*

The Bible was not merely an accumulation of historical wisdom to be memorized and quoted.

MY BIBLE STUDY PLAN

In 1980 I made a commitment to read and study through the entire Bible. This time I committed myself to a fifteen-year plan. For the first five years, I read the Bible in various ways. One year, I used a "read through the Bible in a year" schedule. The next year, I read the Bible in a different translation. Another year, I used an outline of the Bible that listed the passages chronologically (according to historical events) and read it that way. One year, I volleyed back and forth between the Old and the New Testaments.

The second five years, I studied with women's Bible study groups. I also audited Bible classes while my husband was in seminary. When we moved to another state, I joined another women's Bible study group and continued taking classes through a local seminary extension school. Both the groups and classes helped me tremendously to understand the Bible.

I planned to study through the entire Bible on my own the final five years. I wanted to study each passage and write down my own thoughts and understandings. I asked the Lord repeatedly, "How do I accomplish this goal? How do I make it from Genesis to Revelation without abandoning the trip in the middle of my Bible journey?"

At the time I began this intensive five-year study through the Bible, I had three young children. My oldest, Lydia, was in grade school. My middle daughter, Candacee, was a very active toddler. And my son, Andre, had just made his entrance into the world. My husband, after five and a half years of seminary, had just started pastoring a struggling inner-city church. We moved from a small, quiet campus community to a big, noisy city. *Busy, distracted, involved* and *stressed* are only a few words that describe what I was experiencing. I had an overwhelming desire to study through the whole Bible but had very little time, brain space or energy.

Before I got married, I learned an in-depth Bible study method. I used it often in my personal time of study. But when I thought about using this study method from Genesis to Revelation, with all other activities going on in my life it seemed an impossible task. I thought I would be ninety-nine years old before I made it to the end.

I wanted a Bible study plan that would move me swiftly through the whole Bible, give me a quick overview of each passage, but allow me to study deeply. Although I had limited time to study, I wanted that time to give me something relevant to my life to meditate on during the day. Sometimes I would have only twenty to thirty minutes in the morning before the baby woke up.

When I thought about all that I wanted to accomplish in the short amount of time, I knew it was a tall order. Was I asking the Lord for something impossible? When I searched at various bookstores, I didn't see any kind of study method that worked for me. But I kept praying. I knew God wanted me to study, and that he would provide a way for me to do it without the hassle and frustration I was feeling.

One Sunday morning as I was cleaning up the breakfast dishes and getting the children ready for church, the thought came to me, *Think of the Bible as a play.* This was easy to do because I had written several plays based on Bible stories for church programs. A play has characters. It has a backdrop, set or place. It has changes in scenery or characters when major events occur and an overall theme, called the plot. Characters in the play and people who attend the play may not understand certain parts of the drama, such as specific lines spoken or the characters involved. So there may be problems. The playwright's purpose is to convey a message that will change a person's thinking or behavior with some personal application. I was so excited about the thoughts tumbling through my mind that I left the dishes half done and wrote down my ideas.

I played around with this idea for several days until the Lord showed me seven words and phrases beginning with the letter "P" to guide my study. He also showed me how to apply these concepts in Bible study. I believe God gave me insight into a practical way to study the Bible and has continued to give me more insight as I have used this plan to study his Word.

Prepare the passage. An introductory step to get your verses ready to study.

People. Identify and record facts about biblical characters.

Places. Identify, locate and write down the facts about biblical places.

Plot. Write down the main idea or theme of the passage in one or two sentences and make a brief outline.

Problems. Identify and write down words or phrases that are unfamiliar or require more information.

Purpose. Search for and write down the reason God gave you this passage of Scripture to study.

Personal application. Think about and write down how this passage applies to your life and situation right now.

Initially I called this method the "Seven Ps." When the American Tract Society asked to publish them, they changed the name to the "Seven Principles of Bible Study."

When I began this method, I was convinced that the Lord had answered my prayer. I moved through the Bible very easily and quickly. I could study as little as twenty minutes a day, or I could spend a longer time in study; the plan seemed to work either way. It amazed me. I learned so much at such a fast pace. Each day, even if I didn't make it to the personal application part of my study, I would have something to think about and to apply to my life. Because I went through the books so swiftly, I had the confidence that I could make it to Revelation by the end of the five-year period.

It was not long before I started to teach the method in classes and Bible study groups. The women I taught were receptive to this method. It gave them a simple way of studying the Bible. One sister said, "I have heard so many messages and sermons telling me to study the Bible, but I had no idea how to go about it. This method has given me a way to do it." Another woman said, "I used to get up in the morning wanting to have a quiet time and study the Bible, but usually I just sat there reading, not really knowing what to do. Now I know where to start each day and what to do."

I have no idea how many people use this method. The American Tract Society reports that hundreds of the "Seven Principles of Bible Study" tracts are sold each year. The number of people using the method is not important, but what excites me is that more people are studying the Bible.

3

Study! Sisters, Study!

Trying to Make it

*Being a woman in this day and age ain't easy! Feminism and the
women's movement, abortion rights issues, job and sex
discrimination, and plain old daily living often make "walking the
walk" and "talking the talk" very difficult. Being a Christian
African-American woman today is even harder. The plight of
many of our women (unemployment, drug abuse, imprisonment),
problems of our children and youth (teen pregnancy, violence,
substandard education), lack of "eligible" brothers for marrying,
and the high number of single female-headed households often
leave out hearts heavy and our minds burdened.*

*Add to this list the issues of beauty, weight control, sexuality, self-
perception and body-image, loneliness, tiredness, and simply
"trying to make it" in a White male-dominated society, and you
have a glimpse of some of the pressures. . . .*

*[Yet] as we stand and take our rightful place in the power and
spirit of Christ, we will see God do great things through us—for
our families, for our communities, for our churches, for our
nations, and yes, even for ourselves.*

Carolyn Parks, Women to Women

I once heard a preacher on the radio talk about a time he had
to make an important decision about something. He lay on the
floor in his hotel room, and eventually God told him what to

do. I heard this message when I was struggling with doing Bible study each day. I thought, *Hey, I'm going through all this hard work trying to hear what God has to say to me, and all I have to do is lie on the floor.* So for about three days I got up from my bed every morning and laid on the floor listening for God.

The first morning, I heard nothing. The next morning, again, nothing. By the third morning, I sensed God saying, "Get up off the floor and get back to your desk and study! I will speak to you through my Word!"

Now I'm not saying that God never speaks directly to us through this avenue. Quieting ourselves before the Lord and listening for his voice is a discipline believers need to develop. But God's ability to speak to us through his Spirit is not a reason not to study the Word. When God speaks to us directly through the Holy Spirit, our thoughts or other people, we should ask him to confirm the messages through our study of his Word. Sometimes I find myself saying aloud when I'm studying, "Okay, Lord, I get the message. I hear you loud and clear." Our thoughts can be foggy, and the advice of other people can be contradictory, but when we study Scripture the message is a sure thing. He speaks loudly and clearly in his Word. This is one of the most important reasons we study. There are multiple other reasons as well.

To share in the riches of God's kingdom. "What's in it for me?" I have heard many African American women ask this. Many of us come from backgrounds where we have had very little in the way of material possessions. We fall into negative thought patterns, jealousy or coveting what others have. These are sins we need to talk more about. At times that "what's in it for me" attitude comes out toward almost everything we engage in.

So we direct the question at Bible study. We want to know if there will be any personal benefit for what we are doing. I agree that it is a legitimate question. If you are going to spend three hours or more weekly or even as little as fifteen to thirty minutes daily in Bible study, you have a right to ask, "Am I going to get anything out of this?" Many people stop reading and studying God's Word simply because it doesn't seem to address what is going on in their lives. Women lead extremely busy lives, and how we spend our time must hold significance.

I assure you the Word of God is like a treasure chest full of gold. What benefits can we count on from spending time studying the Bible? The longest psalm in the Bible, Psalm 119, is loaded with reasons why we should read, study, meditate on and obey God's Word. Several rich treasures you will receive as you dig deep into the Bible are listed below.

To find our way (v. 5). Although circumstances in our lives may be shaky, if we study the Bible our steps will be firmly planted, our decisions will be sure and our hearts will be clear before the Lord. You come to Christ just as you are. Once he comes to dwell inside of you it's his job to make you like him inside and out. The process is neither easy nor painless. God begins a process of lopping off everything in you that is not like him.

Protection from shame (v. 6). Have you ever talked to a Jehovah's Witness, a black Muslim or a member of some other group with beliefs contrary to Christianity and felt ashamed of your lack of Bible knowledge? The person may have used terms from the Bible you felt you should be familiar with and know how to explain. But you just listened to his explanations and said "uh" and "uh hum." Although some of his arguments made good sense, you knew he was wrong, but you didn't know how to point out his errors. Or have you argued with someone without using the Bible at all? Many times, we don't know the Word well enough to answer arguments in an intelligent way. Often I have been ashamed that I was not able to hurl my sword with precision and accuracy to cut to the truth of the matter and set straight the lies.

Purity (vv. 9, 11). Studying the Word keeps us following the path to godly living. God will let us know when we are traveling into areas that will upset our walk with him.

Counsel (v. 24). God's Word is the best counseling manual on the market, and God, Jesus and the Holy Spirit are the best counseling team.

Discernment (v. 32). So many philosophies and ideas bombard us. It's difficult to know who or what to believe. Studying God's Word gives clarity about what to believe and why.

Hope (v. 49). Hopelessness, discouragement and depression are three things Satan constantly tosses our way. He especially hurls these attacks at women. A consistent diet of Bible study protects one from these kinds of attacks.

Comfort (v. 50). Can I ever testify to this one! In the darkest times in our lives, God makes available his compassion and understanding through the words of Scripture.

Wisdom (v. 42). When we don't know which way to go and what God would have us to do, God's insight is revealed as we study the Word. We can have confidence about the steps we take because we have sought and received his intervention.

Revival (v. 50). Refreshment needed? Need a new start? Time spent in the Bible will give you that fresh start on a daily basis.

Thankfulness (v. 62). Living in America in the midst of vast material wealth, I can easily desire more than what I have. But time spent in God's Word helps me to realize who I am in Christ and how much I already have in him. I come away from my study with a heart full of gratitude, regardless of my circumstances.

Joy (v. 71). The Word of God gives you perspective. You can rejoice and even laugh at the difficulties you are going through because you see things from God's perspective. You are also assured that all things will work out for those of us who love him.

Guidance (v. 105). Are you confused? Need to know which direction to go? The study of God's Word is a road map through life.

MORE REASONS TO STUDY

These are only a few benefits you'll receive from your study. Another major reason to study is found in the book of 2 Timothy. Paul tells Timothy that Scripture is able to equip the believer for every good work. The Greek term for equip is a word used for the setting of broken bones, putting joints in place, mending of nets, and bringing together opposing factions. As we read and study the Word of God, it will serve as a guide, showing us how to build up the body of Christ and to become healers in a world full of hurts and suffering.

Confidence in God's ability. Not only does God speak to me during study times, but also my image of him changes as I study the Bible. When I go through difficult times, I have the tendency to put God in a box. My situation seems overwhelming and I incorrectly think, *Not even God can help me.* As I study

> *But you must continue in the things which you have learned and been assured of, knowing from whom you have learned them, and that from childhood you have known the Holy Scriptures, which are able to make you wise for salvation through faith which is in Christ Jesus. All Scripture is given by inspiration of God, and is profitable for doctrine, for reproof, for correction, for instruction in righteousness, that the man of God may be complete, thoroughly equipped for every good work.*
>
> 2 Timothy 3:14-17
>
> *Be diligent to present yourself approved to God, a worker who does not need to be ashamed, rightly dividing the word of truth.*
>
> 2 Timothy 2:15

the Bible, God begins to grow in size. As I look at his power to open the Red Sea, his ability to protect Daniel in the lions' den and his ability to create a magnificent universe out of nothing with just a word from his mouth, I am forced to let God out of the box. As I continue to study, he no longer fits into my narrow way of thinking.

Searching God's heart. When I study God's Word, I am not just gathering facts for a writing assignment or speaking engagement. I am searching his heart for answers. *Lord, why do I hurt so deeply?* I desperately need and long for God' s embrace, a sense of his constant presence and his words of love and assurance. Personal Bible study is the way he and I move to a deep level of intimate conversation where I receive his love and personal guidance.

I didn't know God very well when I first became a Christian. I was very careful about what I said to him or asked of him. As I have grown in my walk with him, now I understand that I can tell him anything. He already knows all things. Why try to hide when God can read our minds and our thoughts? New Christians are unsure about what might offend God. We rarely express to him our anger, our misunderstandings about his way of doing things or the deepest matters of our hearts.

New believers usually move, in a relatively short amount of time, from casual conversation with God to an intense educational exchange with him. A new Christian might say, "I stayed up all night reading the Bible." This is not out of the ordinary in the beginning of our Christian walk. When believers first come into God's family, they usually have an overwhelming desire to learn. I've been a part of Bible studies that have gone long into the night discussing biblical principles and concepts. Unfortunately, many Christians remain at this level of communication with God. This kind of intellectual approach to the Word of God can go on for a lifetime. The Bible is a fascinating book. One can study its contents forever and always discover new ideas or concepts.

Most Christians do attempt to apply the principles they have learned from the Bible. The Bible says, "Be kind to one another," so you hold the door open for other people. The Bible says, "Be generous with one another," so the next time a homeless person asks you for money, you go to McDonald's and purchase the poor soul a meal.

But God wants us to go to a deeper level of communication. Our heavenly Father wants more than a "See my Word. Now do my will" robotic response from his children. God wants a heart-to-heart connection with us. He wants us to pour out our hearts before him, saying, "Lord, you know everything. I know I can talk to you about my deepest longings and desires. There are no secrets between us. Lord, I long to know you as you know me."

The individual who prays these words wants to know God's heart and seeks diligently to find it. She or he desires not just to receive his physical blessings, but longs to know God and commune with him in a real and intimate way. God knows us inside and out. How well do we know him?

So Jesus, what do you have to say?

4

STINKIN' BIBLE STUDY THINKIN'

THINKING BETTER

Given all that we have to go through, sometimes we say to ourselves like the psalmist David said in Psalm 55:6, after pouring out his pain to God, "Oh, that I had wings like a dove! For then would I fly away and be at rest." With the wings of a dove, we could simply escape. But I want to suggest that it is much more beneficial for us not to run from our pain, but rather to go through it and rise above it.

Attitude determines altitude! The writer of Proverbs says in verse 23:7, "As he [man or woman] thinketh in his heart, so is he [or she]." Psychologists believe that what people think affects their emotions, their ability to relation to others, and the ability to cope in difficult circumstances. What is it that is weighing you down, keeping you from living up to your fullest potential, and hindering you from enjoying the abundant life in Christ (John 10:10)? . . . What you think about it will determine your ability to cope with it.

CYNTHIA B. BELT, *WOMEN OF COLOR BIBLE STUDY*

Has the Bible become like a piece of "church candy?" You know what I'm talking about. Remember when you were little and church services would begin to get long? You'd start to squirm. Auntie or Granny had an old piece of peppermint that had been down in her purse for months. She'd pull it out and take about ten minutes to get the wrapper off 'cause it was stuck on the candy. Half the candy went with the wrapper, but there was still enough to pop in your mouth and keep you quiet for a few more minutes.

Is that like the Word of God? We pop in just enough to keep our anxiety down. We sit and study to keep us still and quiet for a moment. We suck all the juice out, searching for just a few words of encouragement to keep us going one more day. God intended the Word for so much more.

I often start the classes that I teach *to* women *on* women in the Bible by saying, "How to have a relationship with God through the person of Jesus Christ is the primary theme in the Bible. God could have communicated this central idea without specifically mentioning a woman's name. God, however, chose to delicately lace the pages of Scripture with the experiences, faces and names of women. Why? Because he knew that we would be searching the pages of Scripture for women who are like us."

DRINKING IT IN

African American women are in the Word of God. I'm not talking about women of color present in the Bible, though we're found throughout biblical history. (Check out your local Bible bookstore for books about people of color in the Bible. There is even a Bible for women of color; see appendix C for details.) I'm talking about the problems, issues, struggles and dilemmas African American women encounter. They're all over the pages of Scripture. God desires us to see him act on our behalf. Rest assured he comes to our aid as well.

Our attempts to understand how God dealt with women in the

Bible bring us closer to understanding how he chooses to deal with us. As we examine the lives of these individuals, we can recognize patterns and begin to understand God's mind and heart.

WOMEN IN THE BIBLE WITH ISSUES SIMILAR TO AFRICAN AMERICAN WOMEN

	ISSUES	OUTCOME
Tamar	• Raped, discarded after sexual abuse, told to keep quiet, never recovered.	• Realize sexual matters that are unaddressed will sometimes result in major family and relationship problems.
Hagar	• Challenged as a single parent. • Terminated from a job because of child-related issues.	• God sought her out and provided for her needs.
Ruth	• Had misunderstandings with in-laws. • Needed guidance concerning relationships.	• God built a relationship. • Mother-in-law becomes a godly help in relationship resolution.
Esther	• Raised by someone other than her parents. • In need of career guidance. • Fearful and in need of encouragement.	• God provided a godly relative to raise her and give guidance. • God used her significantly.

A MIND CHANGE

One of the first things you may need to do before you ever pick up paper and pen to study the Bible is to change your way of thinking about it. For some the word *study* conjures up negative thoughts, feelings and memories. The word brings to mind a mean teacher carrying a big stick, doing tough homework assignments, reading difficult or boring books, sitting long hours at a desk in a hot classroom or bringing home a bad report card. Studying the Bible may not sound fulfilling or fun.

Once Christ comes to live inside our hearts, we long to know and love our heavenly Father as Christ did. We cannot experience this kind of intimacy with God by merely reading the Bible and studying what someone else has said about it. To grow deeply in a relationship with God requires personal interaction with him through his Word.

In the same way, we bring our attitudes, ideas, motivations and past experiences to the table when we do Bible study. It's important to know and understand what kind of thinking you bring to Bible study.

You may have grown up watching your parents read and study God's Word daily. You saw them consult it for every problem and challenge your family faced. Your parents taught you how to read the Bible and presented it as a fascinating book. You grew to love God's Word. You know its principles and stories well. Reading it is part of your daily life, just like brushing your teeth.

Perhaps you did not grow up with the Bible, but have always been interested in it and desirous to study it. You see Bible study as a challenge and have already tried several methods. You own several Bibles but hardly ever read them because you are too involved in other activities.

Do you have an issue with God? Maybe you lost your mother at an early age and were raised by an uncaring relative. Maybe you were abused or sexually molested as a child, and you've always questioned God for allowing that. Or maybe later in life you went through a bitter divorce or had to deal with a wayward child. In your mind issues continue to present themselves. A sense of agreement and peace with God are still not a part of your thinking. So why should you read and study his Word? Why would you want to hear from someone who seems to have let you down at your darkest hour?

> *We have the tragic, mistaken idea that we must*
> *choose between doing what we want and being happy,*
> *and doing what God wants us to do and being*
> *miserable. Nothing could be further from the truth.*
>
> PAUL LITTLE

When you look at that Bible on your nightstand or coffee table, what do you think? In his letter to the Philippians, Paul instructs Christians about the mindset they should have. Look at the words of Philippians 4:8 in reference to your thinking about Bible study. Be honest with yourself.

> Finally, brethren, whatever things are true, whatever things are noble, whatever things are just, whatever things are pure, whatever things are lovely, whatever things are of good report, if there is any virtue and if there is anything praiseworthy—meditate on these things.

Negative thinking. Usually our minds are set negatively because of past experiences, ignorance, wrong teaching or present difficult circumstances. How do we change our thoughts about Bible study? We need to take a reality check, in light of God's gracious promises and his provision for us.

I've listed below some typical negative thoughts people have as they approach studying the Bible.

I really want to do Bible study, but . . .

- I'm so-o-o-o busy.

PHILIPPIANS 4:8	OLD THOUGHTS	NEW THOUGHTS
True	I don't have time to study the Bible.	
Honest	The Bible is not really helpful to me and my problems.	
Just	It is not fair that God gave others the ability to study the Bible and not me.	
Pure	If I spend all this time trying to figure out this Bible, I'm still going to come away confused. I'd rather read a romantic novel. The Bible is boring.	
Lovely	I read the Bible and life is still a mess.	
Virtue	I follow the Ten Commandments. Isn't that all I need to know?	
Praiseworthy	I was doing just fine in my activities without getting into all this Bible study stuff.	

- I'm too simple-minded.
- I get started and then I fizzle out.
- I need a jump start.
- I'm just plain lazy.
- I'm not convinced it will really help me with my problems.

- The Bible seems so complicated.

- I can't remember what I've read.

- I can't figure out some of these difficult Bible study methods.

- It costs too much. I can't afford any books other than the Bible.

- None of the people I know take time for Bible study.

Ask God to begin to change your "stinkin' thinkin'."

When you first started to drive, it probably felt awkward and unnatural. But now you hop into your car and drive down the road without consciously thinking, *I need to put my right foot here; I must turn on my left turn signal now.* You do those things with ease and familiarity. The same is true with Bible study. For a long time, it may feel awkward and uncomfortable. It may seem like a lot of work with few results. But hang in there. The best is yet to come!

5

No Time!
Help a Sister Out

LEARNING TO SAY NO

One of the greatest combinations of blessings and burdens that black women carry around is the legacy of not being able to say "no." We are socialized to take care of our families, our friends, our communities, and everyone else but ourselves. . . .

Alleviating stress begins with learning to say "no" and recognizing your strengths and limitations. By taking time out to revive ourselves—spiritually, mentally, emotionally, and physically—we are actually doing our loved ones a favor because we are better equipped to attend to their needs. When we are tired, it is harder for our light to shine before others as the Bible commands us (Matthew 5:16). . . .

The very idea of saying "no" drives many of us into hiding with the thought, "I shouldn't be so selfish," or "I can't put myself first. It's not right. They need me." True, putting oneself first is not always right, but rather than automatically saying "yes" to every request, we need to evaluate and determine when "no" is appropriate. Sometimes "no" is the right and healthy answer. Although it will not be easy, we must learn to say it. . . .

Having been programmed to say "yes" all our lives, saying "no" will feel uncomfortable at first. However, as you practice saying it and offering alternatives to the demands on your time and resources, saying "no" will become easier. Others will be taken aback at first, but you will feel better, and ultimately, serve them better.

JETOLA ANDERSON-BLAIR, *WOMEN OF COLOR STUDY BIBLE*

When we say, "I don't have time," we are really saying, "I don't want to take the time" or "My life already feels overcrowded with demands." The truth is found in Ecclesiastes 3:1: "There is a time for everything, and a season for every activity under heaven" (NIV). God has not given us anything to do for which he has not also given us the time in which to do it.

> Our time is in his hands. And it's not our time, it's his.
> We are just putting it back into his hands and asking
> him, "What are we to do with this time you have
> given us?"

Where's the time? Just look at all that needs to be done. The stack of unanswered mail on your desk. The mountain of laundry downstairs. A friend calling in the middle of a crisis who needs to talk. This is your only day off this week. There have been problems in your neighborhood, and there's a community meeting tonight, plus the Wednesday night service at church as well. You begin to panic. You may want to do Bible study, but how will you ever find the time? Let's be realistic!

PRIORITIZING SABBATH REST
We seldom hear a message on sabbath rest anymore. It is a prin-

ciple and a practice that increasingly is ignored. God created the universe in six days, and on the seventh day he rested. Was God tired? No. God never grows weary or tired (Isaiah 40:28). God has established a principle and a practice for us: First you work, and then you rest. Some of us just work, work and work! We don't even remember how to rest.

The sabbath day is an opportunity to worship God, but it also is a time to seek him. On that day, we can take the time to review and reflect on the past week, month, year or our whole life.

We can ask, "Lord, am I going in the right direction? Is there something that I'm doing now that I should not be doing? Is there something that you want me to do that I am not doing?"

If more Christians took time to ask those questions, I believe we would live in a better world. Instead people move like whirlwinds, never stopping to rest or reflect. We block God from providing answers to our problems and solutions to our dilemmas. Using part of a sabbath rest to spend some time to study God's Word is certainly appropriate. (For more information on the concept of sabbath rest, see Gordon McDonald's book *Ordering Your Private World*.)

So teach us to number our days,
That we may gain a heart of wisdom.

PSALM 90:12

A chaotic life. The bottom line about all the things we are involved in is whether we are doing the will of our Father or not. Who was any busier than Jesus? Yet he accomplished everything the Father wanted him to do in thirty-three years. How did he do it?

Observe a chaotic day in the life of Jesus, as recorded in Matthew 14:

- Jesus gets word that his cousin John the Baptist has been beheaded in prison.

- Jesus tries to get alone to deal with this news, but the multitude finds him.

- Jesus sees the great needs of the multitude and has compassion on them.

- Jesus ministers among the people until late in the evening.

- Jesus feeds over five thousand people.

- Jesus sends his disciples away and finishes ministering to the crowd alone.

- Jesus' disciples are out at sea when the weather takes a turn for the worse.

- Jesus walks across the water to see about them.

- Jesus rebukes Peter because of his unbelief.

Yes, this is just one day in the life of Jesus. He can identify with

- losing someone close and dear

- the desire to get away and be alone, but the reality that there are people all around us who have needs

- the tugs at our hearts when we see so many hurting people

How did Jesus cope with a busy, stressful day?	How am I following or not following his example?	How do I need to change my life?
v. 13. He recognized his need for solitude.		
v. 14. He did not see people as a bother.		
v. 14. Although Jesus was hurting and grieving, he was compassionate, not angry, as he met people's needs.		
v. 16. He maximized his time by feeding the people and teaching his disciples a valuable lesson at the same time.		
v. 16. Jesus gave clear instructions that could easily be followed.		
v. 17. He used what he had at his disposal.		
v. 19. He was organized.		
v. 19. He depended on God's power and ability.		
v. 19. He didn't do everything himself but delegated responsibilities to others.		
v. 20. He didn't waste anything.		
v. 23. He spent time alone in prayer.		
v. 25. He didn't let the weather stop him.		
v. 31. He confronted people when necessary.		
v. 34. He rested.		
v. 35. After resting, Jesus resumed his work.		

- having long days
- deciding what to cook for dinner
- having to do so much all by yourself
- bad weather
- being surrounded by people who do not understand you
- having to deal with people who are spiritually immature

How can Jesus' example help you? Fill in the chart on page 48.

Take time this week to evaluate how you spend your time. Ask God to show you where you can spend fifteen to thirty minutes of personal Bible study time with him.

> *The main requirement in learning to study the Bible inductively is the willingness to slow down and really look at what the Scripture is saying. That may not sound too difficult, but in times like ours it is probably the most difficult part of the entire process. And to be honest, my friend, don't you sometimes wonder if our busyness—even for God—isn't often what's keeping us from being what God wants us to be?*
>
> KAY ARTHUR

Making study time a priority. To have time to do the really important things such as Bible study, you will have to drop some of the things you currently do. You may need to reexamine your priorities.

As an African American woman, I challenge you to rethink

your priorities. Get rich? Be famous? Be well educated? Impress as many people as you can? Have as much fun and be as comfortable as possible? Your priorities determine how you spend your time. If you are not spending time getting to know God in prayer and the study of his Word, it is not a priority for you.

In our busy lives, we often misplace our priorities by focusing on what we think is important. Jesus' disciples had the same problem in the time between Jesus' ascension and Pentecost. Perhaps shortly after Jesus ascended into heaven, the disciples each had their own plans—running away to hide, fighting the Romans—but Christ commanded them to wait for his Spirit, and wait they did.

Charles Colson in his book *Loving God* reminds us that as disciples, we too should have the same passionate desire to obey God and to put him first. We really cannot do this very well without knowing the Scriptures. The Bible sets our priorities straight, but first we need to prioritize our lives to make room for Bible study.

Our first priority in life should be loving God. One way we show people love is by spending time with them. How much time do you spend talking with the One who gave and sustains your life?

One way to get your life in order according to God's plan is to set goals for yourself. If we do not know God's plans, purposes and goals for our lives, how are we to find them? The answer is through Bible study. God tells us that he has plans for us (Jeremiah 29:11). God assures us if we call him, he will show us things we do not know and understand (Jeremiah 33:3).

*How do you start your day? Are you a lark or an owl?
Larks twitter and sing in the morning, but by the end
of the day they are not doing too well, they have
slowed down considerably. Owls take a little longer to
get going in the morning—"Right now I don't love
anybody, but when I start loving again, you'll be first
on the list." But owls gain momentum as the night
progresses. . . . Because our individual, built-in clocks
function differently, I've learned that there are no
spiritual brownie points for being a lark. Is it possible
our Heavenly Father created some of us to be larks
and some to be owls so he would have somebody on
the alert all twenty-four hours of the day?*

EVELYN CHRISTENSEN,
WHAT HAPPENS WHEN WOMEN PRAY

Studying requires setting aside time. The Bible study method
in this book can be done daily in fifteen- to thirty-minute segments, or in longer segments of time set aside each week. The
key is consistency. To find the time, you could

- get up a little earlier in the morning if you are not a night
  person

- stay up a little later at night if you are not a morning person

- use some of your Saturday morning sleep-in time

- use some of your Sunday afternoon naptime

Know the best time when you are the most alert.

Studying requires finding the right environment. Prayer is something you can do anytime, anywhere. Bible recordings on tape and CD allow you to listen to God's Word as you commute to work. Scripture verses printed on cards can help you memorize them and meditate on them while you wait in the line at the grocery store or at the dentist's office.

It is impractical to do Bible study on the go, though. Sorry. Bible study is something for which you have to slow down. Studying is accomplished best when a time and a place are specifically set aside for that purpose. The study place should be one where interruptions from family, pets and phone can be limited. Ideally the place should be comfortable and should include a desk or table and writing materials for taking notes, as well as shelves for storing study books.

> *In this world of electronic noise in which telephones, radios, TVs and CDs are creating a constant barrage of sound in our offices, homes and cars, we need to think seriously about preparing a place for study which will afford us the quiet we need to "Be still and know that I am God." ...Since we are careful to make places for our children, our pets and even our memorabilia, how much more should we take care to prepare a suitable place to seek God and to furnish it with all the necessary tools.*
>
> FUCHSIA PICKETT,
> *BECOMING A WOMAN OF GOD*

Here are some examples of places for study:

A portable place

- An old diaper bag
- A cloth, paper or plastic tote bag
- An ordinary box
- A portable file box

A stationary place

- The side of the bed
- A kitchen desk
- A basket in the bathroom
- Your work locker

Just "do it." A commercial on local television advertises a mental health facility called Charter. The commercial ends with "If you don't get help at Charter, please get help somewhere." I have the same philosophy about Bible study. If you don't like the Seven Principles of Bible Study method, please find another method. Don't give up on studying the Bible. Some other method may suit your needs better at this particular time.

What is important is not *how* you study, but that you *do* study. Evaluate your particular needs and situation, and then ask the Lord to help you find an appropriate study. You will probably have to try several different ways to study before you find one that is comfortable for you.

It is important to keep in mind that your study habits will reflect your personality and the particular way God has made you. The Bible lists various spiritual gifts given by God for the building up of his kingdom here on earth. One of those gifts is teaching. I know I have the gift of teaching because I love to do

To everything there is a season,
 A time for every purpose under heaven:
 A time to be born,
  And a time to die;
 A time to plant,
  And a time to pluck what is planted;
 A time to kill,
  And a time to heal;
 A time to break down,
  And a time to build up;
 A time to weep,
  And a time to laugh;
 A time to mourn,
  And a time to dance;
 A time to cast away stones,
  And a time to gather stones;
 A time to embrace,
  And a time to refrain from embracing;
 A time to gain,
  And a time to lose;
 A time to keep,
  And a time to throw away;
 A time to tear,
  And a time to sew;
 A time to keep silence,
  And a time to speak;
 A time to love,
  And a time to hate;
 A time of war,
  And a time of peace.

ECCLESIASTES 3:1-8

detailed research and study in the Bible. I will look up practically every word and cross-reference, and love doing it. It is a reflection of my gift of teaching.

Now a person who has the gift of helps may identify one or two people in the passage, briefly write down a couple of applications and be ready to move on. That is fine, and a natural reflection of the focus of their gift. The Seven Principles of Bible Study plan will accommodate both your personality and your gifts. God will meet you where you are.

6

READY, SET, YOU GO GIRL!

HIP-HOP BIBLE STUDY

Sistas are not too busy to read the Bible. They just do not have an intimate relationship with Jesus Christ—The Man in their life.

Sistas, Bible study is a heart thing not a head thing. We make time to get our hair done, nails and a pedicure, but we can't find time for the Word of God. Then when the "drama" starts we want to call on Jesus.

Girl, you better have some Word in you before you get to calling his name. Show God you love him by seeking his face through the Word of God.

If you got a gossiping spirit and are willing to admit it, Bible study is the best thing that can happen to you. Cause there is some stuff in the Word that you want to tell people about. Girl, they talk about everybody in the Bible, them folks was cutting up back in the day—AD and BC. When I get my Bible study on, I call my sister, my friends and the folks at work and tell them what I heard in the Word. Now, that's some good gossip, girl, cause the Word is true. Ain't lying.

Girl, you want to hear something funny? Every time I make up my mind to study the Word in the morning it seems like I'm up until midnight and too sleepy to get up. If you want some good sleep, just say to yourself I'm going to get up and read God's Word. Girl, sleep will fall down on you like the Twin Towers. That ain't right, but it is true. But the devil's a thief and a deceiver, so set your heart and the alarm clock to follow the things of God, not your mind or your flesh.

Girl, you know I love to eat. Especially when it is that special meal that hits the spot. You know how we get cravings for stuff like

rocky road ice cream, Oreo cookies and shrimp fried rice with
crab rangoons. When I get to studying the Word of God it's like
that special food. It satisfies that craving for more of God.
Sometimes I get so caught up in that thing I cannot eat real food
because I am feasting on the Bread of Life.

JAMIE SAUNDERS (MY SISTA!)

Y ou do what you want to do," a speaker challenged me
when I attempted to use the care of my two young children as
an excuse for not doing more Bible study and prayer. She was
right. If I was preparing for dinner guests I'd make sure the kids
were occupied so I could get the cooking and cleaning done.

At the time I didn't appreciate what the speaker said to me.
The nerve of her implying that I didn't have a desire to do Bible
study! Of course I wanted to read and study God's Word. But after I thought and prayed about it, I realized my time in the Word
and in prayer had more to do with a heart problem than a time
problem. When I had a burning desire to get something done,
I'd find a way—no excuses. So why was it when I said I wanted
to Bible study I wasn't desperately making a way to do so?

I began asking the Lord to give me a longing and a hunger for
his Word like never before. He has to do the work in our hearts
and prepare us to receive what he has for us.

I'm convinced the first place to start with Bible study is not
the materials or the meeting but with our heart preparation.
Pray, "God, may this Word I am about to receive fall on soft
ground, where you can plant." Not just in our minds but in our
hearts.

LORD, PREPARE MY HEART

Don't touch that Bible! Don't turn one single page until you spend at least a few minutes in prayer. Pray! Always pray!

One of my children always greets me when I come home from work, "How'd your day go, Ma?" Another greets me with, "Can I have some money to go to the store?" Now which one do you think I'm glad to see coming?

So many times I've plunged right into the Word without even saying hello to God. As I study, the meaning of verse after verse is like thick molasses. I strain to understand, but the words are heavy and dark. I end up stuck and confused. It is at those times that the Holy Spirit stops me and gently asks, "Victoria, did you pray before you started?"

Prayer is an essential step before beginning Bible study. I strongly recommend that you continue to pray throughout your study. Remember, God wants to speak to you. Feel free to tell him what you don't understand, and expect him to give you clarity.

It may not happen right at that moment, however. Sometimes God will clarify something later as I go through the day or the week. He might use my own thoughts, and like a light bulb turning on, I suddenly understand and the darkness is gone. Or he might use a song, a sermon in church or a message on the radio. Maybe the clarity will come in my study the next day, or maybe not until I study the same passage years later. Prayer is a way to continually say to the Lord, "I'm listening, and I want you to speak to me."

LORD, PREPARE MY MIND

The Bible is not an ordinary book. Its authorship, composition, subject matter, and historical context are truly amazing. How do you see it?

THE BIBLE'S AMAZING COMPOSITION

The way in which the Bible came into being is nothing short of a miracle. Everyone knows the Bible is made up of 66 individual books. But did you know that about 40 different human authors wrote these books? And that they wrote independently knowing almost nothing of the other's part? Furthermore, their period of composition extended over 15 long centuries, three languages and on three continents? Yet, as we examine the Book today, it is one book, not 66. It has a single subject. There is coherence in its content, and progression in its truth.

To see the weight of the argument, suppose you were to endeavor to assemble a comparable book from various bits of literature written since the first century of the Christian era. Take your material from the ancient papyri, pieces of ostraca, writings of the philosophers, ancient wisdom books of the East or anything you choose. Get some writing from every century, select representative material from men in various walks of life; merchants, laborers, priests, farmers. Gather it all together and bind it into one book. Now, what have you? Why, it will be the most ridiculous, contradictory hodgepodge of nonsense you have ever seen.

The Bible, on the other hand, while like that in compilation is wholly different in result. Everything about its composition argues against its unity. There's no reason in the world why it should be one Book. Yet it is, and no honest inquirer will doubt this, if he will take the time to read it carefully.

The human writers of the scriptures had almost nothing in common. Look at their diverse literary qualifications. While Moses may have been somewhat of a man of learning, having been schooled in the best universities of Egypt, Peter certainly was no writer. He was a fisherman, and there is no record that he had any education. Yet the writing of both are saturated with the wisdom of God.

There's one satisfactory answer. Using the ability of these men, or overcoming their disabilities, God spoke through them, and caused that they should write the Scriptures to his divine plan.

BILL BRIGHT, *10 STEPS TOWARD SPIRITUAL MATURITY, BIBLE STUDY*

LORD, PREPARE MY ATTITUDE

In a scene from the movie *Robin Hood: Prince of Thieves,* starring Kevin Costner and Morgan Freeman, the two men are intently fighting their enemies. In the midst of the battle, Morgan Freeman's character reaches for his sword and throws it with one hand with deadly accurate precision, at exactly the right moment, killing one of the people who was about to kill Robin Hood. This amazing dramatic scene made a profound impression on me.

I have seen swords in museums and on a couple of occasions attempted to pick them up. They are very heavy, extremely sharp and difficult to handle. There is no way I could fight with a sword. It is even more ridiculous to think of me throwing one. I'd end up gashing my leg or even cutting off a toe or my foot. I'd probably seriously cut up the people fighting alongside me as well. I can just hear myself saying, "Oh, I'm sorry. I wasn't trying to aim at you! Are you going to be okay?" Mercy! It's best to keep a sword out of my hands. It's too dangerous.

The Bible is described as a double-edged sword (Hebrews 4:12). It cuts deep. It is sharp. Handle with extreme caution, care and skill. Unfortunately, preachers, teachers and other Christians pick up the Word and communicate it to others without first studying. It's used improperly. These people are dangerous.

Handle the Word of God very carefully, like a heavy, sharp sword, especially if you are going to teach it to others. A skilled swordsman spends long hours practicing before attempting to fight a deadly enemy. Our goal as believers should be to become skilled at handling God's Word with accuracy and precision, matching the verses and the principles of the Bible with the needs of people.

> *My church asked me to teach a children's Sunday school class. Immediately, I started taking classes at a local Bible college. I wanted to be sure what I was teaching was correct. I knew God was going to hold me responsible for what I said to those children.*
>
> CLOTTE WARE

When Christians do not properly handle God's Word, the casualties stack up. The wounded lie all around us. Often non-Christians also get sliced up.

Misconstruing passages pertaining to women and slaves is an example of this kind of mistreatment of Scripture. Some passages about women and women's issues are difficult to understand. Therefore they frequently are misinterpreted and incorrectly applied. Just as plantation owners in the early years of American history used the Bible to justify slavery, various denominations, pastors, husbands and others have manipulated portions of Scripture to justify unfair treatment of women and people of color.

LORD, PREPARE ME FOR BATTLE

Paul warns us that our battle is not against flesh and blood (Ephesians 6:12), but against spiritual forces of evil. In the same passage, Paul reminds us to prepare for battle with the full armor of God. We need the "sword of the Spirit," which is the Word of God (Ephesians 6:17).

A sword is used for defense but also for offense. Studying God's Word gives us a strategy not only to defend ourselves against Satan's attacks but to tear down Satan's strongholds here on earth. When Jesus said that "the gates of Hades shall not prevail" against believers (Matthew 16:18) he meant that as we advance on Satan's territory, we will come out victorious. A battle plan against Satan exists in the Word of God. It is there that we find out who we are in Christ and what our Christian life should look like. If Satan can keep us from these truths, he can keep us powerless and ineffective.

Each morning, Satan will send you a memo saying:

Dear Sister,
You have no time to study God's Word today.
I am sincerely yours,
Lucifer

How do you reply to your memo from Satan? Studying God's Word and then applying it will make you one *big* threat to Satan's kingdom. To use an appropriate expression, you can expect all hell to break loose to keep you from it. You will have to fight and persevere to complete the task.

LORD, PREPARE ME FOR THE CHANGES

What do you think Jesus would say if he visited your home or your job on a typical busy day? What changes would he make in your schedule? Do you think listening to him speak to you through his Word would be his priority?

In Luke 10:38-42 we find the answer to those questions. The passage tells us about Martha, a harried woman who had the honor of hosting Jesus in her home. The Scripture allows us to listen in on their conversation:

"Lord, do You not care that my sister has left me to serve alone?" (Mary her sister was sitting at the feet of Jesus listening while Martha was up making all the preparations for the guests.) "Tell her to come and help me!" Can't you just see Martha's hand on her hip (with that "black woman sapharre" stance) as she approaches Jesus?

The Lord answers, "Martha, Martha, you are worried and troubled about many things. But one thing is needed, and Mary has chosen that good part, which will not be taken away from her."

Martha had many problems, just like many African American women do. She did more work than necessary. She told Jesus what to do instead of listening to his instructions. She got caught up in her worries. She thought Jesus didn't care. She saw Mary's choice to sit at his feet as unproductive. Jesus disagreed. He wanted Martha at his feet as well, resting, listening, getting instructions and realizing how much he really loved her.

The original Greek word which describes Martha as "cumbered" (*perispao*) means to drag all around or to distract with care. Many women are loaded down due to past hurts, present difficult circumstances and future worries. They drag around excess baggage on a daily basis. Some barely make it through the day, let alone make time to spend with God in study of his Word. Martha was worried. I can identify with her. It is a constant battle for me. It is also a major waste of precious time. Ninety-nine percent of what we worry about *never happens!*

When my daughter Candacee was seven days old, she had a high fever. Due to her young age, it caused a significant amount of alarm. She had to be placed in the hospital for a series of

tests. The doctors had no idea if she had something as insignificant as a bout with constipation or if she suffered from a life-
threatening disease.

For three days, I was in Candacee's hospital room around the
clock, crying, praying and worrying. Anxious thoughts tum-
bled continuously in my mind. What if it's terminal? What if
this affects her brain and she will never be able to walk? What
if she dies in my arms? What if my older daughter has this mysterious illness too, and I'm going to lose both of them? There
was no end to my worries. I filled my little cot next to Candacee's bed with buckets of tears. Even after she was given a clean
bill of health and was released from the hospital, I still worried
over her in the months that followed. There seemed to be no
end to my anxious thoughts.

Candacee is now seventeen years old. She has a burden for
the salvation of little children, a desire to build an orphanage
in Ethiopia, a beautiful singing voice, and natural speaking
and acting talent. She is the most energetic, talkative and vi-
vacious of my three children. Whenever I need a boost, I go
in Candacee's room and sit on her bed. Before long, she'll have
me laughing, talking or yelling about something. You can't be
in her presence long without her prompting some kind of active response. When I think back on all the worrying I did
when she was ill as an infant, I realize now it was wasted time
and energy.

Like Martha, we often make the wrong choices. We choose
not to spend time and opportunity unloading our burdens at
Jesus' feet. Satan convinces us to take things into our own
hands. God wants to release us from our worries and cares. He
does not come into our lives to place an additional burden on

us. If we sit at his feet like Mary did, we'll sense his love, close-
ness and care. Martha allowed herself to be robbed of a good
thing right there in her own home. What about you?

HIP-HOP BIBLE STUDY TIPS

Bible study can be like a date. I know a few times I have lit
candles, put on my Ben Tankard CD, poured myself a glass of
cranberry juice and opened up the Word of God. Girl, it's like
inviting an old friend over. We get to talking about stuff that
happened back in the day, and we begin to laugh, cry and
repent. I read a few chapters in Psalms to set the atmosphere of
praise, then get some wisdom in Proverbs. The Holy Spirit
comes in and leads you to a passage of scripture. You get caught
in that thing, you start looking up words in the concordance,
checking the Greek and Hebrew, then you find some more
passages of Scripture that line up with the Word. It's on when
you have to get up and get the Amplified Bible. Girl, before you
know it you all up in a Bible study.

Girl, the best part is the meditating on the Word. The music
is soothing, the Holy Spirit is speaking and before you know it
the notebook is full of things to seek on the next day and the
next. Just like all good relationships, you have to put in the
time. Treat yourself; you will not regret getting in the Word. The
Bible got it going on, girl!

JAMIE SAUNDERS

PART TWO

The Seven Principles of Bible Study

7

PREPARING THE PASSAGE

PSALM 139 FOR COLORED GIRLS

Dear Lord, you know me too. Not just mamma and daddy, all my aunts and uncles and cousins—but you know me too. You know what I'm thinking when I get up in the morning and go to bed at night. You even know what I dream about when I can't even remember myself.

You say I can't run away from you. If I try, no matter where I go, you will find me. Even in the darkest night, when I can't find my way, you'll tell me where to go. You're never afraid of the dark.

You say, even before my mother knew she was pregnant, you knit me together. So you gave me this dark skin, nappy hair and big feet. I guess I don't feel so bad about it now. Because you say I am wonderful and you made me very carefully.

And not only did you make me but also you laid out a beautiful life before me to live. Even now you are thinking about how to make me more beautiful inside and out and help me live this exciting life you have planned for me.

You say in order for me to enjoy the life you have planned, I need to let you search my heart. You want to change all negative thoughts I've been thinking about myself.

Next time someone calls me "you old black girl" I'm going to smile, 'cause you are in heaven smiling. One day, when I get to heaven, I'm going to see you smiling at me. But for right now, I'm just going to imagine what you look like smiling down at me everyday and I'm going to think about it all the time.

Thank you, Lord, for straightening me out on all these things. It helps me out a lot.

Your Daughter

I f we start studying in the middle of the Bible or dart around from one book to another, we don't get a whole understanding of what God is communicating to us. I believe every Christian needs to make it a goal at some time to read every word in the Bible and to study every passage, beginning with Genesis and finishing with Revelation. I know. Go ahead and say it: "You've got to be kidding." For some of us, the thought of studying through sixty-six books of the Bible is overwhelming. However, if you have never studied the whole Bible, you have missed tremendous blessings and some very valuable information.

Sometimes I come in the room when my children are in the middle of watching a movie and I start asking, "What happened? Who is that? Why are they doing that?" Those questions exasperate my oldest daughter, Lydia.

"Ma," she says, "you should have been here at the beginning! Too much has happened for us to explain the whole thing."

It was not until I started using the Seven Principles of Bible Study method that I believed studying (not just reading) through the whole Bible was an achievable goal. With this method, I made it through a book of the Bible in a relatively short period and have successfully made it through the whole Bible.

SELECTING A PASSAGE

To learn this method of Bible study, you may want to try working through a smaller book first to get the hang of it. Then you can go from Genesis to Revelation. To teach you how to study the Bible study using the seven practical principles, I have chosen to use the first two chapters of the book of Ruth for our sample study. I chose Ruth because it deals with issues many women face today—relationships, loss, marriage, friendship, loyalty, daily provisions. It is one of the shorter books of the Bible, which makes it easy to illustrate this method and get you started on practicing this method yourself.

> *These [the Bereans] were more fair-minded than those in Thessalonica, in that they received the word with all readiness, and searched the Scriptures daily to find out whether these things were so.*
>
> ACTS 17:11

I will never forget studying the Minor Prophets. Many Christians acknowledge that they have never really studied those shorter books in the Old Testament. I admit it was one of the hardest studies I have ever done. Yet by the end of the study I had experienced the love of God as I never had before. Hosea became one of my favorite books in the Bible. I knew God loved me, but as he opened up my understanding of these books and I saw his love and compassion for Israel, his chosen people, I also felt God's arms coming around me and hugging me in a way I had never felt before. In the minor prophets, you can see God loving his people in spite of their rebellion. It made me think about all my wrong choices and past mistakes. My shortcomings seemed to melt into the sea of his love and compassion.

Preparing the passage

Select a passage of Scripture that is manageable for the time you have. The method described here works best with one chapter or a portion of a chapter at a time. Ruth, 2 Timothy or Philemon are good books to start with.

Read though the entire book in one sitting. If this is not possible, read at least half of the book at one time and then read the other half later. This gives you an overview of where you are going in the book. Some Bible scholars recommend reading the book at least five times before studying it. If you have the time and patience, go ahead. During the first reading, I usually see so many things I want to study that I get anxious to start.

Read the first chapter of the book, marking it as you read. Underline the names of people. Underline the name of each person mentioned in the chapter; these could be a type of person (husband, shepherd, king) or a specific person mentioned by name. Underline only the first reference to the person. I underline the names of God, Jesus and the Holy Spirit every time they occur. Sometimes the names have different meanings, according to the original language and the use in the text.

     ⬭   *Circle the names of places. Circle only the first reference to a place.*

    ?   *Put question marks by words and phrases you don't understand or just want more information about.*

    !   *Put exclamation points by things that are new or exciting to you.*

You can use pens with different color inks to mark the passage. Since pens have a mysterious tendency to walk away from my desk, I use a variety of marks made with only one pen. An example of preparing the text in a part of the book of Ruth is illustrated here.

RUTH 1

1 Now it came to pass, in the days when the judges ruled, that there was a famine in the land. And a certain man of Bethlehem, Judah, went to dwell in the country of Moab, he and his wife and his two sons.

2 The name of the man was Elimelech, the name of his wife was Naomi, and the names of his two sons were Mahlon and Chilion—Ephrathites of Bethlehem, Judah. And they went to the country of Moab and remained there.

3 Then Elimelech, Naomi's husband, died; and she was left, and her two sons.

4 Now they took wives of the women of Moab: the name of the one was Orpah, and the name of the other Ruth. And they dwelt there about ten years.

5 Then both Mahlon and Chilion also died; so the woman survived her two sons and her husband.

6 Then she arose with her daughters-in-law that she might return from the country of Moab, for she had heard in the country of Moab that the LORD had visited His people by giving them bread.

7 Therefore she went out from the place where she was, and her two daughters-in-law with her; and they went on the way to return to the land of Judah.

8 And Naomi said to her two daughters-in-law, "Go, return each to her mother's house. The LORD deal kindly with you, as you have dealt with the dead and with me.

9 The LORD grant that you may find rest, each in the house of her husband."
So she kissed them, and they lifted up their voices and wept.

10 And they said to her, "Surely we will return with you to your people."

11 But Naomi said, "Turn back, my daughters; why will you go with me? Are there still sons in my womb, that they may be your husbands?

12 Turn back, my daughters, go—for I am too old to have a husband. If I should say I have hope, if I should have a husband tonight and should also bear sons,

13 would you wait for them till they were grown? Would you restrain yourselves from having husbands? No, my daughters; for it grieves me very much for your sakes that the hand of the LORD has gone out against me!"

14 Then they lifted up their voices and wept again; and Orpah kissed her mother-in-law, but Ruth clung to her.

15 And she said, "Look, your sister-in-law has gone back to her people and to her gods; return after your sister-in-law."

| 16 But Ruth said:

> "Entreat me not to leave you,
> Or to turn back from following after you;
> For wherever you go, I will go;
> And wherever you lodge, I will lodge;
> Your people shall be my people,
> And your God, my God.

| 17 Where you die, I will die,

> And there will I be buried.
> The LORD do so to me, and more also,
> If anything but death parts you and me."

18 When she saw that she was determined to go with her, she stopped speaking to her.

19 Now the two of them went until they came to Bethlehem. And it happened, when they had come to Bethlehem, that all the city was excited because of them; and the women said, "Is this Naomi?"

20 But she said to them, "Do not call me Naomi; call me Mara, for the Almighty has dealt very bitterly with me.

21 I went out full, and the LORD has brought me home again empty. Why do you call me Naomi, since the LORD has testified against me, and the Almighty has afflicted me?"

22 So Naomi returned, and Ruth the Moabitess her daughter-in-law with her, who returned from the country of Moab. Now they came to Bethlehem at the beginning of barley harvest.

Now you give it a try in your Bible with chapter 2 in the book
of Ruth before you continue reading.

How did you do? How many people did you find? You
should have underlined Boaz (v.1). This is the first time he is
mentioned. Did you find others? Did you remember that people could be types of people? You should have underlined
"reapers" (v. 3), "servant who was in charge of the reapers" (v.
5) and "young women" (v. 8). You may have underlined "young
men" in verse 9. That's okay. I did not underline it because I felt
they were the same as the reapers. As we will see, Bible study
not is only exciting, it is very individualized. For example, I
didn't circle any new places, but you may have circled "field"
since it appears to be outside of the city (v. 18). It is fine if you
circled it.

Now, how about questions and intriguing ideas? I don't expect you to have marked the same ones I did. My marks are
shown below:

RUTH 2

1 There was a relative of Naomi's husband, a man of great
wealth, of the family of Elimelech. His name was Boaz.

? 2 So Ruth the Moabitess said to Naomi, "Please let me go
to the field, and glean heads of grain after him in whose
sight I may find favor." And she said to her, "Go, my
daughter."

? 3 Then she left, and went and gleaned in the field after the
reapers. And she happened to come to the part of the field
belonging to Boaz, who was of the family of Elimelech.

4 Now behold, Boaz came from Bethlehem, and said to the reapers, "The LORD be with you!" And they answered him, "The LORD bless you!"

? 5 Then Boaz said to his <u>servant who was in charge of the reapers</u>, "Whose <u>young woman is this</u>?"

6 So the servant who was in charge of the reapers answered and said, "It is the young Moabite woman who came back with Naomi from the country of Moab.

7 And she said, 'Please let me glean and gather after the reapers among the sheaves.' So she came and has continued from morning until now, though she rested a little in the house."

8 Then Boaz said to Ruth, "You will listen, my daughter, will you not? Do not go to glean in another field, nor go from here, but stay close by my young <u>women</u>.

? 9 Let your eyes be on the field which they reap, and go after them. Have I not commanded the young men not to touch you? And when you are thirsty, go to the vessels and drink from what the young men have drawn."

10 So she fell on her face, bowed down to the ground, and said to him, "Why have I found favor in your eyes, that you should take notice of me, since I am a foreigner?"

\ 11 And Boaz answered and said to her, "It has been fully reported to me, all that you have done for your mother-in-law since the death of your husband, and how you have left your father and your mother and the land of your birth, and have come to a people whom you did not know before.

| 12 The LORD repay your work, and a full reward be given you by the LORD God of Israel, under whose wings you have come for refuge."

| 13 Then she said, "Let me find favor in your sight, my lord; for you have comforted me, and have spoken kindly to your maidservant, though I am not like one of your maidservants."

| 14 Now Boaz said to her at mealtime, "Come here, and eat of the bread, and dip your piece of bread in the vinegar." So she sat beside the reapers, and he passed parched grain to her; and she ate and was satisfied, and kept some back.

| 15 And when she rose up to glean, Boaz commanded his young men, saying, "Let her glean even among the sheaves, and do not reproach her.

16 Also let grain from the bundles fall purposely for her; leave it that she may glean, and do not rebuke her."

17 So she gleaned in the field until evening, and beat out what she had gleaned, and it was about an ephah of barley.

18 Then she took it up and went into the city, and her mother-in-law saw what she had gleaned. So she brought out and gave to her what she had kept back after she had been satisfied.

19 And her mother-in-law said to her, "Where have you

gleaned today? And where did you work? Blessed be the one who took notice of you." So she told her mother-in-law with whom she had worked, and said, "The man's name with whom I worked today is Boaz."

20 Then Naomi said to her daughter-in-law, "Blessed be he of the LORD, who has not forsaken His kindness to the living and the dead!" And Naomi said to her, "This man is a relation of ours, one of our close relatives."

21 Ruth the Moabitess said, "He also said to me, 'You shall stay close by my young men until they have finished all my harvest.'"

? 22 And Naomi said to Ruth her daughter-in-law, "It is good, my daughter, that you go out with his young women, and that people do not meet you in any other field."

23 So she stayed close by the young women of Boaz, to glean until the end of barley harvest and wheat harvest; and she dwelt with her mother-in-law.

PREPARE A NOTEBOOK

I have attempted to do Bible study and keep notes in several different ways. Once I put notes in the margin and blank pages of my Bible. But I found that the margins were too narrow for me to write in. I ran out of blank pages, and it was too messy. When I purchased a new Bible, I lost my notes.

The best thing I have found for Bible study is a three-ring binder. You can add notes continually by adding sheets of loose-leaf notebook paper. If you take a course or a Bible study on a book, you can add your class notes to the binder. Even if you take notes on a smaller sheet of paper or in a church bulletin, you can slip them in plastic page protectors in three-ring notebook size. I label the spine of the notebook, so that when I have to teach, give a talk, or write a lesson from a particular book of the Bible, I can easily find my notes on the shelf.

The notebook system helps me stay organized with my studies, saving me from studying the same material and looking up the same words over and over again. It also helps me remember things God previously taught me from certain passages. In the past, when people would ask me a question and I knew I'd studied that passage but couldn't remember where my notes were, I'd just say, "I know it's in there somewhere." Now I just pull out one of my notebooks and look up what I have studied. If you study the Bible for a number of years, it's quite rewarding to keep adding to your notebooks and seeing God increase your understanding of passages you may not have been clear on when you first began to study them.

PREPARE A NOTEBOOK PAGE

Over the years of using the Seven Principles of Bible Study method, I have learned to set up each page of my notebook with the following information: the date, a page number, and the chapter and verse reference. After dropping pages and being unable to put them back together, or after attempting to remember when I did which particular study, I have found this to be helpful. A sample of a page set up this way is illustrated below.

SAMPLE NOTEBOOK PAGE

1 (page number)   (date)

Ruth 1:1 (Scripture Reference)

Now, if you understand the seriousness and importance of the Word, if you are ready to receive all that God has hidden for you in his Word, if you have prayed, tossed Satan's memo in the trash, gathered your writing materials and prepared your text, then you are ready to begin. Let's go!

8

PEOPLE

THE SISTERS' GIFT

Wise and witty women of Scripture provide us with information, insight and windows of opportunity to view God at work in our contemporized lives. . . . Thank God for women of color who study the Bible. Thank God for the Holy Bible which holds the stories of the matriarchs and patriarchs of our faith. Thank God for continuing opportunities to live our lives in their shadows, to learn from their mistakes, to cry over their plights, to delight in their triumphs, and to be assured by their discoveries of our God who continues to create, use and include women!

DR. LINDA H. HOLLIES, WOMEN TO WOMEN MINISTRIES, INC.

I love testimonies. My faith and my understanding of God are enhanced when I hear a good testimony of how God brought a person through a difficult situation. Studying biblical characters gives us an opportunity to hear testimonies from those people who walked in circumstances like ours.

When I studied the people in the book of Ruth, I discovered that Rahab, the harlot whose story is told in the second chapter of Joshua, also was the mother of Boaz (Matthew 1:5). I had already fallen in love with Boaz the first time I studied him. What a strong, mature, utterly charming character! He was any woman's dream and more. When I looked at the life of Boaz and his mother's history, I knew that no matter what a person's past might hold, God can turn that person's life around and cause good to happen. Not only did God turn Rahab's life around, but also he chose her to be a part of the genealogy of Christ. What glorious things God can do with tainted women who decide to believe in God! I would not have understood this just reading through the Bible, but as I studied the *people* in the Bible, I uncovered this deeper understanding.

While writing my book *Restoring Broken Vessels*, I received many stories from women with damaged sexual pasts. I could tell them with assurance from my study of Rahab, "God *can* and God *will* still use you." God uses women in the Bible, as well as men and children, to communicate wonderful messages to women today.

You already have underlined the names of all the characters in the passage you are studying. Now we will take a step-by-step approach to learning as much as we can about those people. To begin, focus only on the first name underlined in your passage.

Note: We will cover personal application later on in chapter thirteen. But do not think that you have to wait until the end of the study to write down things in your notebook that God speaks to you about. I write "personal note" and jot down what God says to me right in the middle of my notes. I can go back and collect these for the personal application section.

First, *the facts*. Write down exactly what the passage says about the person.

---

1   (date)

People: Ruth 1:

> *v. 1 – judges – leaders who governed during*
> *the time Ruth was written*

Second, *cross-references*. If you have a cross reference, look it up and write down any additional insights you learn about the person. Cross-references usually are found at the bottom or margin of your Bible's pages. If the cross-reference does not give any new information, move on.

---

1   (date)

People: Ruth 1:

> *v. 1 – judges – leaders who governed during*
> *the time Ruth was written*

> **Cross-references:**
> *Judges 2:16-18 – God raised up judges to*
> *deliver them out of the hand of their enemies*
>
> *Judges 17:6 & 21:25 – During the time of the judges*
> *everyone did what was right in their own eyes*

Third, *additional references*. Use a Bible dictionary, study Bible or Bible handbook to look up more facts about the person.

Write down any new information. Use the notes in your study Bible as a last resort, because they are commentaries. Draw your own conclusions first, and read the study notes later to add to what you've learned.

---

1   (date)

People: Ruth 1:

> v. 1 – judges – leaders who governed during
> the time Ruth was written

> Cross-references:
> Judges 2:16-18 – God raised up judges to
> deliver them out of the hand of their enemies

> Judges 17:6 & 21:25 – During the time of the judges
> everyone did what was right in their own eyes

> Additional references:
> History—the first judges in Jewish history were
> appointed at the advice of Jethro, Moses' father-in-law
> (Exodus 18:13-27)

> They were to be God's earthly representatives for justice
> (Exodus 21:6, 22:8; Psalm 82) (Unger's Guide to the
> Bible, p. 525)

Before continuing to read, study the next name listed in Ruth 1 from your Bible and notebook page. Page 86 sets the verse up for you. A sample for comparison is on page 87.

1   (date)

People: Ruth 1:

> v. 2 – Elimelech—(facts from the Scripture passage only)

Cross-references:

How did you do? Remember, yours does not have to look exactly like mine. Your study will be based on the tools you are using.

---

1   (date)

People: Ruth 1:

> v. 2: Elimelech—Naomi's husband & father
> of Mahlon and Chilion
>
> He was an Ephrathite from Bethlehem. He moved his
> family from there to Moab.
>
> **Cross references:**
> Ruth 1:3: He died.
>
> Ruth 4:3: He still had relatives living in Judah that
> had land that Naomi was entitled to
>
> **Additional references:**
> Name means "God is king"

9

PLACES

HOLDING ON TO GOD'S WORD

The Word reminds us of God's goodness. Scripture reminds us that goodness and mercy will follow us all the days of our life and that we will dwell in the house of the Lord forever (Psalm 23:6). Sadly, there are many times when we miss God's blessing by taking for granted the many things that he does for us on a daily basis.

As Christians and especially as African American women, it is crucial for the existence of our very souls to know that every good and perfect gift comes from God (James 1:17). The history of the treatment of women, from the days of being queens in Africa to becoming slaves in America, holds many events in which African American women had only the words of God to hold on to within their hearts.

HANK ALLEN, *WOMAN TO WOMAN*

I once thought the maps in the back of my Bible were there just to add a splash of color to the book. Occasionally, I would look at them with a little more interest if a question in my Sunday school lesson or Bible study lesson asked me to locate a place on a map. Otherwise, I simply was not interested in biblical geography. I thought it was way over my head.

When I started to do the Seven Principles of Bible Study, my attitude changed. As I read and studied each passage, looking at the Bible like a play, I would ask myself, "If I had to choose the furniture or paint the backdrop for this scene, what would it look like?" I soon discovered that looking up information on places added color to my study. I didn't just locate a place on the map, I looked up information on the history and cultural practices of that particular place. It was fascinating. Sometimes what I learned about a place gave me a completely different perspective on the meaning of a passage.

For example, when I studied the book of Ruth and looked up the facts about Moab, Ruth's homeland, I made some interesting discoveries. The Moabites practiced child sacrifice. When Ruth learned that God's people treasured their children as valuable gifts from the Lord and did not kill them, I believe she may have desired to live among this kind of people instead of her own. Previously when I simply read the book of Ruth, I admired Ruth's unselfish desire to go with her mother-in-law to Judah and take care of her. But after reading about Moab and its cultural habits and spiritual rituals, I saw that Ruth probably wanted to escape all of the paganism there and live God's way in Judah, seeking the true and living God.

First, *the facts*. Write down the name of the first place you circled, and list any facts about the place given in the passage.

---

1   (date)

Places: Ruth 1:

     v. 1: Bethlehem—it's located in Judah

Second, *cross-references*. Look up any cross-references given and record any new information on the place or its historical or cultural background.

---

1   (date)

Places: Ruth 1:

  v. 1: Bethlehem—it's located in Judah

  Cross references:
  Genesis 35:16: a little distance from Bethel

Third, *additional references*. Look up the place in a Bible dictionary, Bible handbook, Bible encyclopedia or additional scriptural references. Write down in your notebook any new information you discover.

---

1   (date)

Places: Ruth 1:

  v. 1: Bethlehem—it's located in Judah

  Cross references:
  Genesis 35:16: a little distance from Bethel

  Additional references:
  Genesis 35:19: burial place for Rachel

  Matthew 2:1, 5-6: birthplace of Christ
  name means "house of bread"

Fourth, *geographical location.* Locate the place on a Bible map or in a Bible atlas. Note anything significant about its geographical location (for example, on the coast, in the mountains, desert terrain).

Obviously, people and places aren't the focus of every passage you'll study. In those cases, just skip these categories and move right into plot.

Now you try with the next place listed in Ruth 1 in your Bible. A sample is found below.

---

1   (date)

Places: Ruth 1:

> *v. 1: Judah—in the times of judges there was a famine*
>
> ***Cross references:***
> *none listed*
>
> ***Additional references:***
> *Genesis 29:15-35: son of Jacob & Leah; their*
> *descendants' name means "let him be praised"*

10

PLOT

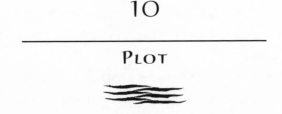

GOD'S WORD IS LIKE ICE CREAM IN THE SUMMERTIME

When I tell people about the joy of Bible study, some understand immediately. Others look at me in disbelief and say, "Does it really take all that?" One woman saw all of my Bibles and books spread out over the table where I was doing my study and said, "This is just too much."

I smiled and said to myself, Honey, you just don't know. My early attempts at studying the Bible were like eating bran cereal. Someone told me it was good for me that it would help me grow as a Christian, so I tried it. Like the bran cereal, I knew the value of it, but I didn't necessarily like it. I ate it anyway. I began to study the Bible out of sheer obedience. In those first few years, if someone had asked me about my Bible study habits, I would have said, "It takes a lot of hard work!"

And it was. It was a lot of hard work fighting Satan to get to the study. It was more work attempting to use some of the Bible study materials I had purchased or people had given me. It was even more difficult trying to understand what God was trying to communicate to me. It took still more effort to apply biblical principles to my personal situation and to try to change some of my ungodly behaviors. Bible study required more effort than I had bargained for, but I kept at it, determined not to go down in defeat. Now spending time in God's Word is like eating ice cream in the summertime: refreshingly delicious. I can't get enough.

VICTORIA JOHNSON

The plot of a story, play or movie is a short, concise explanation of what it is all about. If someone were to ask you what *Romeo and Juliet* is about, you might tell them, "It's a love story about two people who wanted to get married but their families opposed the marriage so they married in secret; then they died." In one or two sentences, you've summarized what happened. In the same way, to summarize the plot in a chapter of the Bible is simply to tell what the passage is all about in one or two sentences.

For example: Genesis 1 is about God creating the universe in seven days. Psalm 23 is about the Lord being our shepherd and the ways in which he provides for us. Hebrews 11 lists the great men and women of faith in the Bible, briefly explaining what they accomplished for God.

Read the Bible with an open mind. Don't try to straightjacket all of its passages into the mold of a few pet doctrines. . . . But try to search out fairly and honestly the main teachings and lessons of each passage.

HALLEY'S BIBLE HANDBOOK

When you think through and then write out the plot of a chapter, you are more likely to remember what the passage is

all about. After a while, you will remember where certain passages are in the Bible and won't have to fish though the whole
Bible for the information.

Look again at Ruth 1. How would you summarize the plot?
What kind of action is going on in the chapter? Is it a love story,
a conflict, a battle or a conversation? Who is involved? How
does it conclude?

Here is an example of a plot summary for Ruth 1.

1   (date)

Plot: Ruth 1:

> This is an account of a woman named Naomi returning
> to Judah from Moab, and how she deals with her two
> daughters-in-law.

Now try it with Ruth 2.

1   (date)

Plot: Ruth 2:

> Naomi's daughter-in-law Ruth goes to glean in the fields
> when they return to Bethlehem. She meets Boaz, a wealthy
> man related to Elimelech who protects and makes special
> provision for Ruth.

In this step, you may also want to include an outline of the
passage. Look at the passage you are studying like a play or a

skit, and picture in your mind the different scenes. Like the plot, your brief outline should get to the point. This might be easy if you have a Bible that already divides the chapters into sections. You have the option of using those divisions, which I often do when I study, or to divide the passage up in a way that makes sense to you. Outlining the chapter also helps you to remember the events in the chapter.

Here is a sample outline:

---

1   (date)

Ruth 1: Outline:

> v. 2-5: Naomi moves from Judah to Moab and her husband and sons die there.

> v. 6-15: Naomi decides to return to Bethlehem.

> vv. 16-20: Naomi's daughter-in-law Ruth returns to Bethlehem with her.

11

PROBLEMS

THE GIFT OF ALONENESS

When we are lonely, it may mean that we have not yet learned to enjoy our own company. We have not yet realized the gift of aloneness.

Everyone needs time to be alone. Aloneness is an investment. It is time to recharge one's emotional and spiritual batteries; time to think and pray; a time to gain insight or find a solution to a pressing problem; rest after a battle or a long day; time to find grace to deal with life and all of its challenges; and time to hear from God.

Jesus took full advantage of his singleness and moment of aloneness or solitude. Mark 1:35 says, "In the morning, rising up a great while before day, he went out and departed into a solitary place, and there prayed."

It is when we are alone and still that God can speak to us most profoundly. Did He not tell the psalmist as recorded in Psalm 46:20, "Be still, and know that I am God?" We all need moments of aloneness to hear from God, reflect, meditate, and recreate.

CYNTHIA L. HALE, *WOMEN OF COLOR BIBLE STUDY*

The Bible is not a simple book. You've got a woman clothed with the sun in Revelation 12. A woman praised for putting a spike in a man's head in Judges 4—5. What do these fantastic stories mean? Can the average Christian hope to understand complex words and events in the Bible? Using Bible study tools, each of us *can* find answers in the Bible without holding a seminary degree.

When you initially read through the passage, you put a question mark by those words and phrases that you did not understand or that you wanted to gain more insight about. To study those words and phrases, follow the three-step method.

First, *the facts.* What does the passage say? Is the word in question used more than once in the chapter? What is the context?

Second, *cross-references.* Look up the word or phrase in a Bible dictionary or other reference, and briefly record your findings.

Third, *additional references.* Look up the word or phrase in another resource such as an encyclopedia, a book on the manners and customs of the Bible, or a book on difficult biblical passages, such as *Hard Sayings of the Bible.* Record any new information you glean.

Here is an example of problems in Ruth 1.

---

1   (date)

Problems: Ruth 1

> v. 4: married Moabite women—Were the Israelites allowed to marry Moabites?
>
> Moab was outside the tribal territory of Israel (see places; you should have already researched Moab).

Is there a cross-reference for this word or phrase? Write down what you learn.

---

1   (date)

Problems: Ruth 1

> v. 4: married Moabite women—Were the Israelites allowed to marry Moabites?
>
> Moab was outside the tribal territory of Israel (see places; you should have already researched Moab).
>
> **Cross-references:**
> Deuteronomy 23:6: friendly relations between Moab and Israel were discouraged but not forbidden.

After consulting additional references, record any new information you glean on your notebook page. See the sample below and check how you did.

1   (date)

Problems: Ruth 1

> v. 4: married Moabite women—Were the Israelites allowed to marry Moabites?
>
> Moab was outside the tribal territory of Israel (see places; you should have already researched Moab).
>
> **Cross-references:**
> Deuteronomy 23:6: friendly relations between Moab and Israel were discouraged but not forbidden.
>
> **Additional references:**
> The Israelites were not to intermarry with certain foreign tribes. The Moabites were one of the forbidden tribes (The Bible Almanac, p. 415).

Now you try one. What other words or phrases did you mark with a question mark? Write down one of them in your notebook and follow the three steps to gain more insight. How did you do?

Here is a sample of another problem in Ruth 1.

1   (date)

Problems: Ruth 1

> v. 15: her gods—the god in Moab and the God Naomi
> served in Judah were different

> Cross-references:
> Joshua 24:15: Joshua challenged the Israelites to either serve
> God or the god of the surrounding heathen nations.

> Judges 11:24: Chemosh is the god of the Moabites.

> Additional references:
> Chemosh: Solomon built a temple for this god on a
> mountain east of Jerusalem. This was one of the reasons
> for his downfall.

12

PURPOSE

STAYIN' ON TRACK

God's Word warns us of danger and directs us to hidden treasure.

Otherwise how will we find our way?

Or know when we play the fool?

Clean the slate, God, so we can start the day fresh!

Keep me from stupid sins, from thinking I can take over your work;

Then I can start this day sun-washed, scrubbed clean of the grime of sin.

PSALM 19:13 THE MESSAGE

$\mathcal{S}$ex. Why does God limit such a natural drive to marriage? Those of us who have experienced sex outside of marriage know why. The consequences, the hurts, the broken relationships that result from premarital or extramarital sexual relationships can be excruciatingly painful. The best sex and the best way to experience sex is inside the confines of a committed marital relationship. God always has a purpose in mind when he prohibits certain behaviors. God's teaching on sex comes through clearly in the pages of Scripture. And in the same way that there is a purpose behind how God created us as sexual beings, there is purpose to all of Scripture.

Certainly, God did not write the Bible aimlessly. When he inspired the various writers, he had a message to communicate. He wasted no words. As we study his Word, we must ask, "What did God have in mind when he wrote this passage? Why did he prohibit one thing and allow another?"

Many times when people attempt to interpret the Bible, they start here, with this principle of purpose. Before studying the passage closely, they are ready to say what they *think* it means or what they *think* God is communicating. Shame on them! The passage should always be studied carefully and thoroughly before drawing any conclusions about what the Author is trying to say.

Correspondence always has purpose. God's written communication to us has purpose. Whenever we sit down and write another person, we have a thought or idea we want to communicate that we hope will cause a certain response or action. People seldom write without purpose or meaning. Consider the purpose of the following letter from a grandmother to her granddaughter graduating from college:

My darling granddaughter,

I love you. And I want you to know that even if you had not gotten your degree, my love would have been the same. Whether you are on the mountaintop or down in the valley, my love will always meet you there.

You are our first to take that walk across the stage and re-

ceive that precious printed paper that will open the door to so many opportunities for you. You are our first to graduate from college. You are our first to attend an institution full of the culture of our people. Spelman College and you were a perfect match. And I'm so glad you had a chance to be under the influence of Johnetta Cole before she moved on. What a mentor of strength she was for you and the other women at Spelman.

I'm writing this note to let you know we are so proud of you. I rest assured that you will continue to make our family and me proud of your accomplishments from this day on. In whatever way I can help you to further your education or your career, I want you to know I am here for you.

Your loving grandmother

This grandmother wrote her granddaughter with several definite purposes in mind. First, she wanted to communicate how proud she and the family were of the granddaughter. Second, she wanted to communicate her love for her granddaughter. And third, she wanted her granddaughter to know that she was available to continue to help her along in her future endeavors.

Your word is a lamp to my feet
And a light to my path.
(PSALM 119:105)

What if this letter were found several generations later by a great-great-great-granddaughter? By that time, Spelman College may have merged with another college and have a new name. While we in this generation know that Johnetta Cole was the president of Spelman College for many years, the great-great-great-granddaughter probably has no clue who Johnetta Cole was. She might make some assumptions without going to her computer to look anything up. Perhaps she'll assume Spelman was an insignificant little college and that Mrs. Cole must have been one of the teachers. Instead of being impressed that her foremother received a degree from a major African American college, she might flippantly think, *One of my relatives went to college. So what?* But if she took a few minutes to do a bit of research on even the name of Spelman College, she would get a totally different picture of what her ancestor had accomplished.

Often we make quick assumptions about God's Word. Because we don't do the study, we do not get the full impact of the message God is delivering. Once we study the people, places and plot, we should understand his purpose for writing the passage.

> *If purpose is not known, abuse is inevitable.*
> **MYLES MUNROE**

First, *the facts*. See if the text clearly states the purpose for the passage, or if it contains a key word, phrase or verse. This may already be stated in your plot summary.

Second, *review.* Look back over your study for ideas or clues as to why God may have wanted us to study this passage. As you write down the ideas, it is good to put the verse reference by each point. This way you will know that you are not just making up an interpretation but that it is grounded in the passage.

Third, *interpretation.* Answer the question, "Why did God write this?" as clearly as you can, based on the facts in the passage and your study. Record your answers.

Finding the purpose of a passage will help you understand God's perspective and will prepare you for the seventh principle of personal application.

The following is an example of stating the purpose of the passage, from Ruth 1:1-14:

---

1   (date)

Purpose: Ruth 1

> v. 1-5: to show that hardships and difficulties can affect God's people

> v. 6-13: to show that in the midst of pain and grieving, one can make sound decisions as Naomi did

> v. 14: to show God's care for widows; God gave Naomi a committed daughter-in-law

---

Now you try stating the purpose of Ruth 1:15-22 in your notebook. How did you do?

1   (date)

Purpose: Ruth 1

> v. 17: to show Ruth, a heathen, despised by Israel; to show
> that a Moabite can still make a decision to follow and devote
> herself to the true and living God

> v. 20: to see Naomi's honesty about her difficult times
> and bitter feelings

13

PERSONAL APPLICATION

HELP FOR HARD TIMES

Several years ago, when I was going through a rough time (one of those typical "Black woman things!"), I was studying the book of Leviticus. I thought that perhaps I should switch books until this trial was over and go back to my study in Leviticus later. I was very doubtful that God could speak to me at this time of difficulty when I was going through page after page of Old Testament laws and rituals. God, however, seemed to encourage me to keep studying where I was. And sure enough, God began to speak to my specific situation through the book of Leviticus.

I had never paid much attention to the Old Testament laws pertaining to women. But as I read and studied them, I heard God say, "I understand women. I know about your hormonal changes, your monthly cycle, your emotional makeup and your need for time to recover physically and emotionally after childbirth. And because I made you and I understand you, I have put some guidelines in place just for you." God even gave guidelines for the treatment of foreign women and children who came into the Israelite camp after being captured. God commanded that they be treated gently and fairly. This really spoke to me as an African American woman who sometimes feels like a foreigner in America. As I studied this, I heard God speaking to me about my present difficulty. "I know you. I made you. I understand the hormonal changes you are going through. I will be gentle with you. I will guide you. I will not ignore your spiritual, physical or emotional needs."

VICTORIA JOHNSON

When I worked on a summer youth program in Detroit, Michigan, the director of the program, Haman Cross Jr., taught me a valuable lesson about Bible study. I complained to him about the study we had chosen to do for the summer. I told him that it did not seem to be meeting the needs of the women in my discipleship group. Most of the women in the group were single African Americans, grappling with unhealthy relationships, having questions about their future, facing racism on their jobs and so on. I wanted to switch to another book in the Bible.

Haman wisely said, "Make a list of your needs, and as you study, ask the Lord to meet your needs and make the present study relevant to your situation." I applied that principle to the group study that summer, and I was humbled to see God begin to speak to our deepest needs right there in the passage we were studying at the time. I began applying this new principle to my personal Bible study as well. It's amazing how God answers us where we are. He happens to know when we will be studying what book at certain times of our lives, and he promises to speak to our situations through his Word.

The principle of personal application is one of the best parts of Bible study. By the time I have thoroughly studied the text, God has revealed many things to me about my particular situation. Throughout the study I write down the things God seems to be saying specifically to me. I'm afraid that if I don't, I will forget them by the time I get to the personal application part of the study. Even if I do forget, it's okay because there are always several other points of application to write down at the end.

Remember the question, "What does this have to do with me?" It is one of the excuses many of us give for not doing Bible study. The Bible seems like a dusty old book with stories about foreign people who lived in ancient times. It does not seem to scratch us where we itch. We don't expect it to minister to our deepest needs and hurts. In our instant society, we want quick answers and easy self-help formulas to solve our problems. Sometimes what God says to us in the Bible is totally different from what we *think* we need.

Frequently, as I study, I hear God speak to me clearly through the passage, "I am here for You. I love you. I care for you." These words are not specific answers to my problems, but they are what God knows I need to hear at the time. Sometimes I just have to go through something in my life without a lot of answers as to why it is happening and what comes next. But when I hear my heavenly Father say, "I am here and I will take you through," it is enough for me.

> But be doers of the word, and not hearers only, deceiving yourselves.
>
> JAMES 1:22

Ask yourself the following questions to be sure you have given the Holy Spirit the chance to use the Bible to make a difference in your life each day.

• How does the passage apply to me?

- Are there attitudes I need to change as a result of my new understanding?
- Are there warnings that I need to heed?
- What principles did I find that I need to live by?
- What do I need to begin doing? What behavior do I need to change or stop?

The Scriptures were given not to increase our knowledge, but to change our lives.

D. L. MOODY

Personal application is the most exciting part of my Bible study. I usually look back at the purpose and ask myself personal questions. Sometimes prayer will come after I write out a personal application. Many times I will write out a short sentence or statement to God.

Also, as a Bible teacher one of my main goals is to make the Bible relevant to African American women. It's at this point in my study that I usually get the most help for my sisters who are often facing several challenges.

On the next page is an example of a personal application from Ruth 1. In your notebook write out any personal application that you have discovered from Ruth 1.

In order for our Bible study to make the desired change in our lives, we have to be honest, practical and quick to respond in the personal application phase of Bible study. For instance, in the example on page 111, I list the people God brings to mind.

1   (date)

Personal Application: Ruth 1

vv. 1-5: Am I believing I should never encounter any trials as a Christian? I need to accept both good and bad times as part of living in this world.

vv. 6-13: Do I make sound or emotional decisions in the middle of a crisis? Lord, help me!

v. 14: Do I see God's provision and help through others or am I always trying to work things out on my own? Lord, thank you for helpful family and friends.

v. 17: Have I given up on any believers being converted? Lord, bring to mind those who may have had bad times as part of living in this world.

v. 20: Are there some bitter or angry feelings that I need to confess to God and others? If so Lord, bring these to mind.

We have looked at the first two chapters in the book of Ruth using the Seven Principles of Bible Study. We have approached it from the perspective of people, places, plot, problems, purpose and personal application.

Now it is time for you to tackle the remainder of the book on your own. We all know that practice makes perfect. One teacher went on to say, "Practice makes permanent." God's Word is so good, so personal and so applicable for busy women today. This method will not work unless you take the time to use it. The more you use it, the more it will become part of your life.

I mentioned that I chose the book of Ruth because it dealt with many issues that women today deal with, especially African American women: relationships, marriage, grief, moving, in-laws and daily provisions. These issues are the realities of our lives, the distractions that hinder us from having time to study the Bible. *Come on, my sisters, no more excuses!*

APPENDIX A:
LEADER'S GUIDE

TEACH OTHERS

African-American women . . . must follow the way of Jesus and give love to all kinds of people. Amazingly, when love is given, love somehow is returned. It is not always returned from those to whom it is given, but it will be returned. Jesus will see to it. At various times in my life, I have given love to nursing home residents, housing project residents, shut-ins, groups of teenagers, children and disabled persons.

In each instance, I have met regularly with them, shared gospel devotions or Bible studies, given gifts, shared myself (my feelings, thoughts, and activities), taken them on outings, and planned parties. Inevitably either those with whom I shared, or their relatives and friends, have become my friends and have filled my life with love.

. . . So often women allow competition, jealousy, suspiciousness or ill will to dominate their relationships with other women. As a result, they miss the richly loving relationships that women can have with other women. If African American women would only form support groups, Bible study groups, fellowship groups, and prayer groups with other women who face similar concerns, they would find that loving relationship will begin.

DR. JACQUELINE TILLES, *WOMAN TO WOMAN*

As I travel, I'm encouraged by the number of women who are brave enough to start a small group study. The material in this book can easily be implemented as part of a Bible study or Sunday school series. The study can be completed in twelve weeks. Simply follow this guide. Feel free to combine or expand the lessons if you have more or less time.

Suggestions for Leaders

If you are a veteran adult group leader who has led multitudes in studies such as this before, this leader's guide can still be helpful to you. Simply skim the suggestions for each session and choose what may aid you in your personal study.

If you are a brand new leader, doing something like this for the first time, relax! Pick up a good book on leading small groups. See the list of resources for leaders at the end of this section.

Be as well acquainted with the lesson and the Scriptures in the lesson as possible. The more thoroughly you prepare, the better the study will be.

You may want to have the study at someone else's home. That way the host can tend to preparing the place for the study and serving refreshments (if you plan to have any) afterward. Your sole responsibility will be leading the lesson. (Caution: keep food to a limit. Many times in circles with African American women, food becomes a big thing. Women who attend and the hostess at times may start to prepare big, elaborate meals instead of spending time preparing for the study. Let God's Word be the main soul food and save the fried chicken for another occasion.)

Be enthusiastic. If you are not, your group will pick up on your lack of interest and leading the group will become like dragging around a basket of wet towels.

Few pastors understand why parishioners are not always eager to attend church on weeknights, pursue extensive home Bible studies or participate in door-to-door evangelism. Very often the person employed in the business world comes home and barely has enough strength to open the front door! In essence, an average Christian's lack of interest in church activities may simply be the result of sheer exhaustion, not diminished sainthood.

Use teaching aids as much as possible, such as an overhead projector, chalkboard or colorful markers and large sheets of newsprint on an easel.

Encourage the group members to bring their Bibles to each session. It is good to have several modern language translations and paraphrases on hand for purposes of comparison.

Start right by starting on time. This will set the pattern for the rest of the sessions. Stop on time also. Going overtime discourages women from attending meetings. Give them the option of staying longer and talking if they like. Be sure to clear this with the host beforehand.

Begin with prayer. Ask the Holy Spirit to open hearts and minds and to give understanding so that the truth will be applied.

Involve everyone. Group involvement is a key to learning.

Promote a relaxed environment. Arrange your chairs in a circle or semi-circle. This promotes eye contact among members and encourages more discussion that is dynamic.

*"Teaching the Bible can be fun!" These words came
from the lips of a nineteen-year-old student who had
just completed her first try at teaching a short Bible
study. She had been scared at the prospect. But her
plan had worked. . . . Now the ordeal was over. She
was relaxing at the table where only a few minutes
before she had been teaching her lesson. Everyone
had left but her, her partner, and me. As she relaxed,
she again repeated, "I did not realize that teaching
the Bible could be so much fun!" I asked her what she
meant by fun.*

*"It was such fun," she answered, "to see the eyes of
the students light up and their faces break into smiles
as they discovered some of the things we had
discovered in our study." In this first attempt, she had
discovered the joy of teaching discovery Bible study.
While there are a variety of joys a teacher might
experience, there is a special thrill in seeing the lights
go on in students' eyes as they begin to discover some
things for themselves in a passage of Scripture.*

*Now it is true that not all teaching is a joy.
Sometimes teaching can be frustrating and
discouraging. Many have tried being a teacher and
have found it so discouraging that they quit. One of the
paradoxes of teaching is that it can be both satisfying
and frustrating, depending on circumstances,
responses of the students, the kind of teacher
preparation, and methods used. Teaching has the
potential for both agonies and ecstasies. Any veteran
teacher knows that no session plan is foolproof.
What will work with one group may not work at all
with another.*

LORETTA WELD, *THE JOY OF DISCOVERY IN BIBLE STUDY*

Be relaxed in your own attitude and manner. As the leader, be sure to address people by name to help others get acquainted.

Stick to the lesson topic. Avoid time-consuming tangents.

Encourage the participation of every member in the group. Discourage domination of the group by a compulsive talker or someone who "knows it all."

If a question comes up that you cannot answer, do not be afraid to say to the group, "I'm not sure about this, but perhaps we can all try to find the answer for next week." Or assign the question as a project to one volunteer.

Do not allow commentaries in the group. They may keep group members from searching and thinking for themselves.

Expect God to bless your efforts.

For each session, you will probably need

- a chalkboard or an overhead projector. Newsprint and markers also work.
- extra Bibles for those who may not have one.
- a copy of the book *The Sisters' Guide to In-Depth Bible Study* for each person.
- several Bible dictionaries. You may need to borrow references from your church library or ask people in your group to bring some to share. If you purchase several inexpensive Bible resources, some group members may want to buy them from you for their own study.

LESSON 1: GET ACQUAINTED

To prepare:

- Bring a 3" x 5" card for each person in the group.
- Ask one person to share their personal testimony about their journey to successful personal Bible study.

> *We who are "shepherds" [leaders] must not expect*
> *our "flock" [group] to take time to study the Bible; we*
> *must motivate them to do so. Many former pastors*
> *admit that they now have as much difficulty as any*
> *layman in getting to prayer meeting.*
>
> *Therefore, the Christian leader must project an*
> *aura of excitement concerning deep Bible study. The*
> *only way to do that is to get excited ourselves, and*
> *then share with our congregation [group] the reasons*
> *why we are excited. The great task for today is*
> *producing men and women of the Word, Christian*
> *workers whose fellowship and ministry reflect the one*
> *truly relevant Book of the ages!*
>
> **GRANT R. OSBORNE AND STEPHEN B. WOODWARD**

- Print 2 Timothy 2:15 on a piece of paper for each person (*optional*).
- Study 2 Timothy 2:15 and define these key words: *study, approved, workman, ashamed, dividing* and *truth.*

When the group meets:
- Have each person write down three things about themselves on a 3" x 5" card, along with a brief statement about why they are taking this particular study. Then ask each person to share those things with the group. You may want to jot some notes or keep the cards. As you go along in the study, the initial comments of group members will help you tailor the lessons to ensure the needs identified are being met.

- Ask someone in or out of the group who has discovered the fulfillment and joy of personal Bible study to share her experience. Make sure she shares both the negative and positive aspects of their experience.
- Read 2 Timothy 2:15. This is the theme of the book. Have each group member look up one of the key words. If the group is large, break up into small groups and assign each group a word. Ask them first to tell what they think the word means, second, to look it up in a Bible dictionary and discuss the definition, and third, share what they find with the whole group when you get back together.
- Allow a few women to share what they learned at the meeting that they were not aware of before they came. Emphasize that this is what Bible study is all about. As they study at home in preparation for the group meeting and as they study together as a group, God will open up their understanding of his Word and of himself.
- Assign chapter one to be read before you meet again the next week.
- Conclude with each woman giving a sentence or two in prayer asking God to meet the needs she mentioned at the beginning. The leader closes in prayer for each individual (if the group is small enough).
- Remember to begin and end on time.

LESSON 2: FEASTIN'
To prepare:
- Read chapter one.
- Think about a time you used Bible study to help you though a crisis. Or maybe if you are new to Bible study,

think of a time you should have turned to the Word rather than things like food, other people or depression. Be prepared to be honest with the group.

When you meet:
- Be sensitive to the fact that the introduction to the book could have brought up hurtful experiences for the women.
- Allow them to briefly share their experiences but remember this is a Bible study and not a support group. Always bring the discussion back to the question, "How did the study of God's Word help you?" Or "How do you think it could have helped you instead of what you turned to?"
- Break up into pairs and have the women pray for each other and their Bible study habits. Ask them to be specific about areas they need to change.
- Assign chapter two for next week.

LESSON 3: BEATIN'
To prepare:
- Chart your cycle of Bible study habits.
- Look at each of the Seven Principles of Bible Study and make sure you have a basic understanding of each one.

When the group meets:
- Put the cycle of defeat from pages 22-23 on the board before the members arrive. Ask if anyone can identify with this cycle. Ask each woman or, if it's a large group, a few women, to tell what their Bible study cycle is like.
- Discuss what the author did to break out of her cycle of de-

feat. (She kept at it, she was determined, she discovered the Author behind the book, she studied with a group, and she asked God for a simple method to help her in her study.)

- Break up into small groups. Assign each group one (or more) of the seven principles. Ask each group to share (1) their understanding of that particular principle; (2) an example of the principle from anywhere in the Bible; and (3) how this principle could be helpful to them in understanding the Bible and the God who reveals himself through the Bible.
- List three main reasons for studying the Bible, according to the author of this book. Discuss them and then list the reasons why the group members want to study the Bible.
- Assign chapter three for next week.
- Close in prayer. Ask God to search their hearts about their failures at Bible study and their renewed desire to do it now. Pray for pure motives. One of the group members or the leader should close in prayer for the whole group.

LESSON 4: STUDY! SISTERS, STUDY!

To Prepare:

- Take time this week to read through Psalms 139 and 119.
- Read "Psalm 139 for Colored Girls" in chapter three and highlight points that are touching or relevant to you.
- Highlight the values from Psalm 119 (pages 31-33) that you are hoping to pursue as you go through your time of study.

When you meet:

- Have someone who reads well read Psalm 139 from the

Bible and "Psalm 139 for Colored Girls." Use that as an opening prayer.

- Talk about how this psalm ministered to you. Give the other ladies a chance to talk about it as well.
- Divide into groups and have each group look up one or two promises from Psalm 119. Have them discuss what we can expect to gain from studying the Bible, according to these verses. Ask how they think this will benefit their lives personally.
- Assign chapter four for next week.

LESSON 5: STINKIN' BIBLE STUDY THINKIN'
To prepare:

- Think through your own times of negative thinking about Bible study. What changed your negative thinking to now wanting to lead a group to help others study? Be prepared to share your testimony or have someone you know who has a testimony like this talk about their experience.

When the group meets:

- Put three headings on the newsprint or chalkboard: "Study," "Bible Study," "Personal Bible Study." Ask the group members for the first thing that comes to mind when they hear the word *study*. Jot down their answers in the first column. Then ask them about "Bible study" and "personal Bible study."
- Break up into groups and give each person or group a list of passages to look up from the riches of God's Word.
- Assign chapter five for next week.

LESSON 6: NO TIME! HELP A SISTER OUT

To prepare:

- Bring a sheet of paper for each group member.
- Study Matthew 14. What was Jesus' stressful day like, and how did he handle it?
- Review your pattern of time spent with God. Repent if necessary and be prepared to be honest with the group about your times of inconsistency or struggle with time in God's Word.
- Study Ecclesiastes 3.

When the group meets:

- Give each person a sheet of paper and ask them to write down a description of their most hectic day and how they handled it.
- Break into two smaller groups. Let one group discuss worry and the other sabbath rest. Ask the group to discuss the helpful suggestions the author gives. Regroup and share the suggestions with each other.
- Have them write down the different times and places Jesus met with his heavenly Father.
- Read the quote from Evelyn Christensen on page 51. Ask each person to explain where they plan to do their study and at what time.
- Pray together specifically about the times and places people plan to have their study this week. Ask God to meet them there in a special way. Look together at the list on page 48. Review how Jesus handled stress so that we can get an idea of how we should handle it. How can you apply it to your life? (Talk on the phone while washing dishes, give children clear instructions and delegate responsibilities, accept of-

fers of help, get organized, depend on God to help you, pray, deal with anger, recognize your need to be alone.)
- Assign chapter six for next week.

LESSON 7: READY, SET, YOU GO GIRL!
To Prepare:
- Study Luke 10:41-43.
- Are you more like Mary or Martha? Jot down your reasons why and be prepared to share with the group.

When the group meets:
- Have some members of your group act out Luke 10:41-43.
- Allow the group to discuss whom they are most like, Mary or Martha.
- Discuss Jesus' reaction to Martha and how that is relevant to us today.
- Assign chapter seven for next week.

LESSON 8: PREPARING
To Prepare
- Set up a page in your notebook as an example for the group.
- Be ready to give a general explanation about how to mark a chapter for study (see pages 72-73).

When the group meets:
- Show your prepared notebook. Allow other women who have their notebooks ready to show them and share tips with each other.
- Read the entire book of Ruth. Let each woman take a paragraph at a time.

- Assign chapters eight and nine for next week.

LESSON 9: PEOPLE AND PLACES

To prepare:
- Study the people and places of Ruth 1. See chapters eight and nine in this book.

When the group meets:
- Ask if anyone in the group has ever written a play or skit on a story in the Bible. Ask them to share how they did it. Was it difficult or easy?
- Review pages 88-89, which refer to the Seven Principles of Bible Study as parts of a play. Ask the group to pretend that they are sitting in the audience and the characters in the Bible are acting out the scenes.
- Read through Ruth 1 and give instructions about marking the passage. Point out the example in the book. Assure them that you will take time with the passages next week.
- Break into small groups. Ask each group to list the main places and characters in the book. Allow the women to share the facts they discovered about the people and places.
- Come back together as a large group and ask the members to share: what they have learned so far, what has been most exciting and how they have been able to apply learned material to their personal situation.
- Assign chapters ten and eleven for next week.
- Close with a time of thanksgiving. Ask God for continued clarity and understanding in his Word. Stress that we are not just studying to say we are studying, but we are studying to get to know the Author of the Book.

Lesson 10: Plot and Problems
To prepare:

- Identify the plot of Ruth 1—2. Review chapters ten and eleven in this book.
- Research the words and phrases you marked with question marks. Be ready to show your group what steps you took in your research.

When the group meets:

- Ask if anyone has seen a movie or a play lately. Ask them what it was about. They will probably say what kind of movie it was, make mention of the main characters, and generally tell what it was about. Point out that they just explained how to summarize a plot.
- Read Ruth 1 aloud. Have each person write down in one or two sentences what Ruth 1 is all about.
- Break into smaller groups and figure out the play-by-play action of Ruth 1. Come back together and share conclusions. Then list all the words or phrases marked with question marks. Review how to go about finding out more about each problem word or phrase.
- Assign each group member a word or phrase to research at home. Also assign chapters twelve and thirteen for next week.
- Close in prayer.

Lesson 11: Purpose and Personal Application
To prepare:

- Research and write down the purpose for Ruth 1. List as many personal applications as you can.

When the group meets:

- Share homework assignments. Don't stop at answering the problems, but give the group members time to talk about the negative and positive aspects of their personal study time.

- Read the grandmother's letter from pages 102-3. Explain how it relates to Bible study. She was trying to communicate a specific message. God communicates a specific message. The member of a later generation misunderstands because she did not take time to study. Our generation often misses the point God is trying to make because we fail to study.

- Read through Ruth again. Break up into small groups and ask them to list as many of God's purposes for writing this book as they can. After each group lists the purposes, have them go back over their lists and see if they can make personal applications. Get back together and compare notes.

- Think about what you've learned and be ready to share on Sharing Day.

LESSON 12: SHARING DAY

- Have fun on this last day. Allow each person to share what she has learned in the study. Ask them to keep their comments brief so that everyone has a chance to share. A simple meal or light refreshments on this final day might be appropriate.

Appendix B:
Choosing a Bible Version

Translations	Features	Reading Level	2 Timothy 2:15
King James Version	• Poetic literary style using Elizabethan English • A well-loved and accepted translation • Most difficult to read	12th	Study to shew thyself approved unto God, a workman that needeth not to be ashamed, rightly dividing the word of truth.
New King James Version	• Easier to read and understand than KJV • Modern language in elegant literary style • Growing in popularity	8th	Be diligent to present yourself approved to God, a worker who does not need to be ashamed, rightly dividing the word of truth.
New American Standard Bible	• Easy reading • Considered by many scholars to be the most accurate translation available	11th	Be diligent to present yourself approved to God as a workman who does not need to be ashamed, accurately handling the word of truth.
New International Version	• Bestselling modern language translation • Enjoyed by a wide range of denominations	7th	Do your best to present yourself to God as one approved, a workman who does not need to be ashamed and who correctly handles the word of truth.
Good News Bible (Today's English Version)	• Modern language • Praised for its freshness of language	7th	Do your best to win full approval in God's sight, as a worker who is not ashamed of his work, one who correctly teaches the message of God's truth.

TRANSLATIONS	FEATURES	READING LEVEL	2 TIMOTHY 2:15
The Living Bible	• A popular, readable paraphrase • Used by many for easy reading	8th	Work hard so God can say to you, "well done." Be a good workman, one who does not need to be ashamed, when God examines your work. Know what His Word says and means.
Contemporary English Version	• Uncomplicated English used in our daily lives. • Appropriate for the entire family • Gender-inclusive language	5th	Do your best to win God's approval as a worker who doesn't need to be ashamed and who teaches only the true message.
The New Living Translation	• Easy to understand	6th	Work hard so God can approve you. Be a good worker, one who does not need to be ashamed and who correctly explains the word of truth.
The Message	• Paraphrase in everyday language	8th	Concentrate on doing your best for God, work you won't be ashamed of, laying out the truth plain and simple.
New Revised Standard Version	• Easier to read than the RSV • Gender-inclusive language	8th	Do your best to present yourself to God as one approved by him, a worker who has no need to be ashamed, rightly explaining the word of truth.

Appendix C:
Resources

Studying requires making an investment. If a plumber came to your house without a box of tools, you would question his competence. Many of us claim to know God's Word, teach it and try to live by it, but we do not own one study tool other than the Bible. Anyone who is serious about understanding his Word must invest in Bible study tools.

African American women are willing to invest money to look good on the outside. Are you willing to invest just as much to look good on the inside?

The following tools and aids are suggested for Bible study. Of course you do not need to rush out and purchase every item on the list today. Use this as a guide to slowly build a good study library.

Study Bible. Purchase a good study Bible. They come in various versions. Study Bibles usually have some or all of the following: introductions to each book, explanatory notes, articles, maps, dictionary, concordance and topical index.

The Thompson Chain-Reference Bible. This thorough and helpful work has a host of notes in the margin and an excellent "condensed encyclopedia" section divided into more than four thousand topics. It also contains information on the canon and the principal English versions, an outlined analysis of each book, a number of maps, a concordance and an index. This Bible also has a good harmony of the four Gospels and several excellent charts.

A concordance. One of the foremost tools for Bible study, a concordance provides immediate access to any Scripture verse by reference to only one word or a few words contained in it. *Strong's Exhaustive Concordance, Cruden's Complete Concordance*, and *Young's Analytical Concordance* are probably the most popular.

A Bible dictionary or encyclopedia. A Bible dictionary is an alphabetically arranged compilation of words, like an ordinary dictionary, but lists those words with biblical significance. Included are proper nouns of the names of persons and places, as well as common nouns with scriptural meanings. A Bible encyclopedia serves a similar purpose, with expanded information.

The *New Bible Dictionary, Unger's Bible Dictionary, The Bondservant Pictorial Encyclopedia of the Bible* edited by Merrill C. Tenney, and the *Expository Dictionary of Bible Words* by Lawrence Richards are just a few of the good dictionaries on the market.

A Bible atlas, biblical history books, and books on Bible manners and customs are not essential but can be very helpful to the Bible student. An atlas helps the student visualize the settings of the events of Scripture. It gives general information on Bible geography, geology and archeology, often containing colored and outlined maps and photographs of biblical places. *The Moody Atlas of Bible Lands* and *Baker's Bible Atlas* are both good choices. Books on Bible manners and customs shed light on the culture of people in biblical days. Other good choices include

The IVP Bible Background Commentary: Old Testament and *The IVP Bible Background Commentary: New Testament.*

A Bible handbook is a valuable tool for study. Those who do not wish to invest in a number of books can substitute it for other reference books. *Halley's Bible Handbook* and *Unger's Bible Handbook* have both been around for a long time and are excellent tools.

A Bible commentary comments on the Bible passage-by-passage and verse-by-verse, interpreting the meaning.

Commentaries should be consulted only *after* completing one's own study. Bible scholars have recorded the results of their studies in these books. Some commentaries are the work of a single author, while others are a compilation of the efforts of a number of authors. Commentaries may range in size from one volume to well over fifty volumes.

Three better known commentaries are *Matthew Henry's Commentary on the Whole Bible*, *The Wycliffe Bible Commentary* and Warren Wiersbe's "Be" series of *Bible Exposition Commentaries*.

This list is by no means exhaustive. Your pastor or Bible study teacher may be able to direct you to other materials or tell you how best to use the ones listed above. Grant Osborne and Stephen Woodward, in their book *Handbook for Bible Study*, make several helpful suggestions for building a personal Bible study library:

Purchase your library over a period of time. Use birthdays or Christmas as an opportunity to receive materials. If you are studying with a group, you sometimes can get a discounted price if you order several copies of a book all at once.

Make good use of a Christian library. Churches, seminaries, Bible colleges or retreat centers may have libraries that are open to the public. Call around in your area.

Organize your buying. Make a list to take with you to the bookstore and stick to it.

Choose the better books. We are always looking for a bargain, but the less expensive study book may not be the better one. Do compare prices, however. Sometimes ordering from a mail order catalog is cheaper, but be sure to consider the cost of postage.

Choose works that are true to the text. Check whether an author has used the original languages, rather than writing only from his perspective.

> *When I get a little money, I buy books, and if any is left, I buy food and clothes.*
>
> DESIDERIUS ERASMUS

SMALL GROUP HELPS

Arnold, Jeffrey. *The Big Book on Small Groups*. Downers Grove, Ill.: InterVarsity Press, 1992.

Briscoe, Jill, and Laurie Katz McIntyre. *Designing Effective Women's Ministry*. Grand Rapids, Mich.: Zondervan, 1995.

McBride, Neal. *How to Have Great Small-Group Meetings*. Colorado Springs: NavPress, 1997.

———. *How to Lead Small Groups*. Colorado Springs: NavPress, 1990.

ADDITIONAL BIBLE STUDY HELPS

Arthur, Kay. *How to Study Your Bible*. Eugene, Ore.: Harvest House, 1994.

Jensen, Irving L. *Independent Bible Study*, rev. ed. Chicago: Moody Press, 1992.

McQuilkin, J. Robertson. *Understanding and Applying the Bible*, rev. ed. Chicago: Moody Press, 1992.

STUDY BIBLES

The New Inductive Study Bible. Eugene, Ore.: Harvest House, 2000. Created by Kay Arthur's Precept Ministries. This Bible doesn't tell you what to think, it teaches you how to think and how to discover Bible truths for yourself through inductive study.

The New King James Study Bible. Nashville: Thomas Nelson, 1982. Has 5,700 annotations on biblical teachings, events and personalities. This Bible also includes doctrinal footnotes, the latest information on archeological sites, detailed book instructions and outlines.

The Original African Heritage Study Bible. Nashville: J. C. Winston, 1993. Cain Hope Felder, editor. Reveals the history, lineage, and influence of African people in Scripture and show how Africans contributed to the formation of Judaism and Christianity. Highlights passages about black Bible people, paintings from Cameroon's Mafa Tribe, spirituals and slave songs.

Women of Color Study Bible. Iowa Falls, Iowa: World, 1999. Highlights people of color in the Bible and has women's devotionals that pertain to women of color and their situations.

The Full Life Study Bible. Grand Rapids, Mich.: Zondervan,

1992. Includes a charismatic systematic theology and theme finders that link significant texts in the Pentecostal tradition. Same page application notes stressing victorious life in the Sprit. Seventy-five study articles on subjects important to charismatic believers.

Hebrew-Greek Key Study Bible. Chattanooga, Tenn.: AMG, 1990. It brings out the meaning and grammatical significance of the major Hebrew and Greek words and keys them to Kohlenberger number system. Also cross-referenced to Strong and Kohlenberger's *Dictionary of Hebrew, Aramaic and Greek*.

The Open Bible. Nashville: Thomas Nelson, 1983. Has 4,500 notes, 300 word studies keyed to *Strong's Concordance*, and an 8,000 subject Biblical Cyclopedic Index. This Bible comes in the King James and New King James versions.

Life Application Study Bible. Grand Rapids, Mich.: Zondervan, 1997. Includes dictionary/concordance, book instructions, applications and study notes, harmony of the Gospels and profiles of Bible people.

The Student Bible. Grand Rapids, Mich.: Zondervan, 1994. For young adults and new Christians. Features updated book instructions, optional reading plans, valuable study articles, a guide to "100 People You Should Know" in the Bible and a listing of well-known biblical events.

APPENDIX D:
POETRY EXAMPLE

PREPARING THE PASSAGE

? SONG OF SOLOMON 1:1-5

1 The song of songs, which is <u>Solomon's</u>.

2 Let him kiss <u>me</u> with the kisses of his mouth—?
?   For your love is better than wine.

3 Because of the fragrance of your good ointments, ?
!   Your name is ointment poured forth;
   Therefore the <u>virgins</u> love you.

4 Draw me away!
   We will run after you.
   The king has brought me into his chambers.
   We will be glad and rejoice in you.
   We will remember your love more than wine.
   Rightly do they love you.

5 I am dark, but lovely,
   O <u>daughters of Jerusalem,</u>
   Like the tents of Kedar,
   Like the curtains of Solomon.

1   (date)

People: Solomon 1

> v. 1: Solomon—the third king of Israel, David's son, author
> of Proverbs, Songs, and Ecclesiastes.
>
> **Cross-reference:** Solomon wrote 3000 proverbs and 1005
> songs. Song of Solomon is believed to be one of them.
>
> v. 2: Me—refers to Solomon's bride. She is talking about
> the king.
>
> v. 3: virgins, daughters of Jerusalem—same. The attendants
> to the bride and then to the new wife. Virgins, young women
> around the palace to serve the queen, also could be the
> women in Solomon's harem or can sometimes refer to all the
> women of Jerusalem.

1   (date)

Places: Solomon 1

> v. 4: Chambers—bedroom, inner room, wedding chambers, private place in the house.
>
> **Cross-reference:** Psalm 45:14-15

1   (date)

Plot: Solomon 1

> King Solomon writes a song and his bride desires his kisses and admires his love, oils and name. The maidens also admire him.
>
> **Outline**
>
> v. 1: Introduction
>
> vv. 2-3: She desires his kiss and admires his love and oil
>
> v. 4: She is brought into his chambers and desires to run with him

1 (date)

Problems: Solomon 1

v. 1: Songs—Song of Songs, the most excellent song, singing. A poem.

v. 2: Love—beloved, friend, relation

v. 2: Kisses—mouth to mouth, touching, attached, this is a kiss among lovers

Kisses were common among lovers, friends, fellow countrymen, and relatives.

Cross-reference: Song of Solomon 4:10—Your love is better...

v. 3: Oil—grease, liquid, usually refers to olive oil, prepared for various purposes, sacrifices in worship, cooking, anointing future offices holders (kings and priest)

Your name is like purified oil—Purified oil is transferred from one bottle to another.

Cross-reference: Ecclesiastes 7:1—a good name is better than a good ointment.

1   (date)

Purpose: Solomon 1

Purpose of the book is to see our relationship between Christ and his bride the church. Solomon represents Christ and the bride represents us.

Purpose of 1:1-4: to see the desire, admiration and intimacy on the part of the bride.

1   (date)

Personal Application: Solomon 1

v. 2: The man takes the initiative; she waits for him and desires for him to kiss her.

In my relationships with the opposite sex, do I allow the man to take the lead? Do I observe and obey this as God's instructions for how relationships should be handled?

In my relationship with my groomsman Christ, am I a patient bride and allow the Lord to lead and move the relationship to a more intimate one in his timing? Or am I demanding?

1 (date)

Personal Application: Solomon 1

v. 2: The bride saw intimacy as better than wine or outside substances.

Do I want intimacy with Christ at all costs or am I still looking for things outside of Christ to please and satisfy me? Do I see his love as something that is greatly desired?

v. 3: Solomon's fragrance was appealing but his inner character was also appealing. His name was better than purified oil.

Do I admire Christ's qualities and desire them for my own? Do I value the name of Christ?

v. 3: Other people besides Christ's bride recognized his qualities and loved him.

If I am in a relationship with someone of the opposite sex do other people admire and love him as well as I do?

v. 4: Once again she is wanting and allowing him to be the initiator. She says "draw me after you." She desires for the two of them to run together.

1   (date)

Personal Application: Solomon 1

Am I desiring Christ to draw me closer? Do I want to run with him? Or am I running ahead or behind him?

v. 4: The king has brought me into his chambers.

Have I come to a most intimate place with God? Do I desire to draw him into all my secret places and allow him to share his secrets with me?

v. 4: Once again the women of Jerusalem are approving and rejoicing about this relationship.

If I am in a relationship with another person, are my family and those around me pleased? Why or why not? Could this be a warning for me that the relationship is not a positive one?

ABOUT THE AUTHOR

Victoria L. Saunders Johnson was born in Joliet, Illinois, to James and Mattie Saunders. She is married to Curtis Johnson and is the mother of three children—Lydia, Candacee and Andre. She is a freelance writer and editor, and has taught at the Moody Bible Institute Extension in Milwaukee for ten years.

Victoria has been a staff member of Campus Crusade for Christ. She also worked at Detroit's Afro-American Mission. She counsels and disciples many women and coordinates various women's ministry activities. She is presently teaching "A Woman's Walk Through the Word" at St. Paul's COGIC Church. Victoria travels and teaches nationally and internationally on women's Bible study, sexual issues and emotional pain.

Victoria is also presently working with several social service agencies in the African American community, including Sojournah Truth House (a domestic-violence agency), CareNet of Milwaukee (a crisis pregnancy center), Bethany Christian Services (sexual abstinance program) and New Horizon Center (a group home for boys).